Dear

Happy
Travels!
love,
Susan &
Julia

Judy Watten

YUNNAN

Patrick R. Booz

PASSPORT BOOKS

Trade Imprint of National Textbook Company
Lincolnwood, Illinois U.S.A.

Published by Passport Books in conjunction
with China Guides Series Ltd.

This edition first published in 1987 by Passport Books, Trade
Imprint of National Textbook Company, 4255 West Touhy
Avenue, Lincolnwood (Chicago), Illinois 60646-1975 U.S.A.

In Lijiang: Rock's Kingdom reprinted by permission of Deborah Rogers Ltd.

Printed in Hong Kong

Series Editors: May Holdsworth and Jill Hunt

Photographs by Magnus Bartlett (32−33, 72, 76−77, 80, 82−83, 104−105, 110, 112−113,
116−117, 120−121, 136−137, 141, 157, 184, 186−187, 192, 194−195, 207);
Patrick Booz (4−5, 20−21, 40−41, 44, 85, 109, 133, 152−153, 180−181, 202−203);
Zhang Jing (16−17, 56−57, 60−61, 68, 96, 190−191); Mao Baige (124−125, 144−145
148−149, 183, 198−199); Ingrid Morejohn (160, 170−171, 174−175, 177);
Hao Yaojin (12−13, 28−29, 48−49, 86−87); China Guides Series (9, 64−65);
Tom Nebbia (100−101, 166−167); China Photo Library (8); James Montgomery (92−93);
Ren Qin (162−163); Herman Wong (179)

Maps and artwork by Unity Design Studio

Contents

Names and Addresses

In this book addresses are given in *Pinyin*. *Lu* is a road and *jie* is a street; *xiang* is a lane or alley.

Names of hotels and restaurants are also given in Chinese characters in the text to help visitors getting about on their own. Names of all the sights and other places described in the book are given in Chinese characters in the Index of Places.

Yunnan Province

Yunnan is the sixth largest of China's 27 provinces, similar in size to California. It contains more variety than any of them, with towering, icy mountains adjoining Tibet and Burma in the northwest and lush jungles bordering Laos and Vietnam in the south. Half of all China's animal and plant species can be found somewhere in Yunnan, and its 33 million people include members of 24 different ethnic groups — a third of its total population.

Geologically, Yunnan is an offshoot of Tibet, whose soaring tableland spreads eastwards, creating a plateau of red earth over a mile high (about 2,000 metres). Yunnan's southern latitude, astride the Tropic of Cancer, combined with its high altitude, gives it a gentle climate. Winters are mild and sunny; summer brings cool monsoon rains.

In western Yunnan the mighty ranges of the eastern Himalayas fan south from Tibet's border, channelling some of southern Asia's greatest rivers through immensely deep canyons. The Salween, the Mekong and the Yangzi (Yangtse) race side by side far below the snow-capped peaks, barely 80 kilometres (50 miles) apart. Movements in the earth's unstable crust continue to thrust the mountains upwards and subject Yunnan to periodic earthquakes.

Fertile lake basins lie in geological faults on the plateau. These form the agricultural, political and cultural heart of the province. Kunming's Dianchi Lake is the largest. The red soil produces rice in abundance, along with year-round vegetable crops, and teas that are considered to be among the best in China.

Botanical gardens in Kunming and in tropical Xishuangbanna display an amazing array of plant life. Many valuable herbs, staples of Chinese medicine, originate in the mountains. Botanists come to see the camellias and rhododendrons, the province's special pride, since all species of these splendid shrubs trace their ancestry to Yunnan. Wild animals and birds also exist in geat variety. Elephants and tigers, though rare, still roam the jungles near Laos and Burma. Bears and snow leopards are sometimes seen in the eastern Himalayas. Sadly, many rare animals are being hunted to extinction for their fur or for those parts that are valued in medicine.

Yunnan has a very long history. Mankind first appeared at least a million — or perhaps as much as three million — years ago. For many years Peking Man, discovered in 1921, was the oldest known example of prehistoric man in China — until geologists began planning the Kunming-Chengdu railway in 1965 and saw Yunnan's fossils. An old cowherd from the village of Yuanmou, northwest of Kunming, mentioned that villagers had been grinding up 'dragon bones' as medicine for years. The surveyors, recognizing the local name for fossils, found a deep gully near Yuanmou whose cliff-like walls contained quantities of ancient mammal fossils. Among them, a young geologist discovered two human front teeth.

Paleontologists from China's Academy of Sciences named this ancient man *Homo erectus yuanmouensis*, or Yuanmou Man. The formation of the teeth convinced them that he was Peking Man's ancestor, China's oldest known humanoid. Later excavations in 1973 indicated that Yuanmou Man knew the use of fire, and shared a lakeside plain with primitive forms of elephant and an early ancestor of the horse, extinct species that helped to date him.

A million years or more passed with no record to show how Yunnan became populated or how its people lived. For the first thousand years of China's recorded history, it was known only as a savage region inhabited by non-Chinese tribes, beyond the reach of Chinese civilization. In 1955 a sophisticated Bronze-Age culture was discovered when 48 untouched tombs, dating from 1200 BC, were found at the southern end of Lake Dianchi (see page 54). These ancient people, living in a kingdom named Dian, described their daily life in great detail, using bronze figurines to depict miniature scenes on the lids of their huge treasury vessels. The people of Dian were slave-owners and head-hunters; they took part in an animal cult featuring bulls, reminiscent of their close contemporaries in King Minos's Crete; the Dian folk also practised advanced methods of agriculture and were fine artists as well.

The first recorded Chinese invasion was in 339 BC, when a prince of the Yangzi River Valley sent his general over the mountains to conquer the 'southwest barbarians'. The campaign lasted ten years, during which his return route to China was cut by the prince's rivals. When the general found himself isolated, he set himself up as the King of Dian in a capital near present-day Kunming. For two centuries his descendants ruled the kingdom, completely cut off from China, and intermarried with the Dian people.

The great Han Dynasty ruled China from 206 BC to AD 220 and struck up an important silk trade with Europe. Citizens of the Roman Empire quickly developed a taste for silk togas. One branch of the Silk Road ran through Yunnan to India. The Han emperor, wishing to control the entire trade route, launched the second Chinese invasion of Yunnan. The King of Dian welcomed the invaders, hoping his new allies would help him to subdue neighbouring tribes. He thereupon received an imperial seal recognizing Dian as a tributary state. But the Chinese army could not get past Yunnan's formidable western mountains and eventually withdrew. Dian's tribal chiefs ruled in the name of the emperor and when the Han Dynasty finally collapsed, Yunnan continued on its own course as before. In time, the Dian kingdom weakened and tribes from the south seized power.

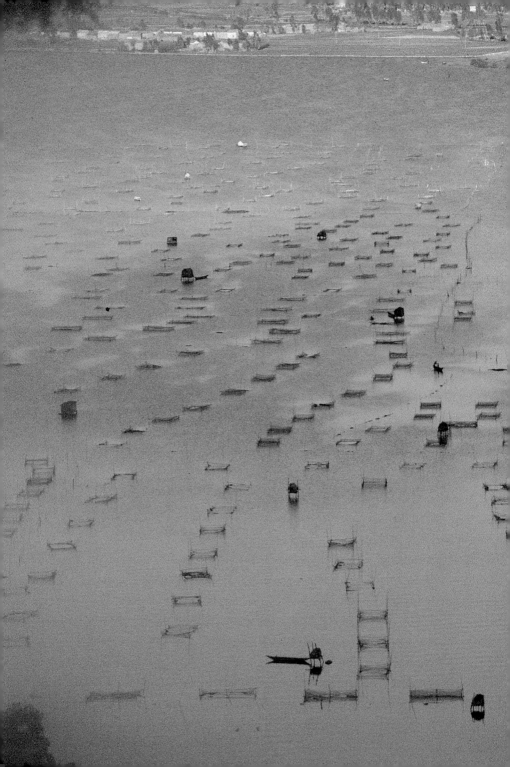

In the eighth century, six princes ruled the southwest. One of them is said to have travelled north to China, which was enjoying a golden age under the Tang Dynasty (618−907). When asked where he came from, the prince replied that his home was south of Sichuan's rainy weather — at which the emperor dubbed the land Yunnan, meaning 'South of the Clouds'. (This tale is disputed by some historians, who claim that the Han emperor chose the name many centuries earlier.)

In 732, the most ambitious prince treacherously invited the other five to a banquet. When they were suitably drunk, he set fire to the wooden banquet hall, killing them all. The triumphant prince seized their lands and named himself Nanzhao — Prince of the South. For five centuries, the Nanzhao Kingdom and its successor, the Kingdom of Dali, remained strong and independent, on a par with China and Tibet, its warring neighbours. Its capital was Dali, on Erhai Lake in western Yunnan.

The kingdom came to an end in 1253 at the hands of Kublai Khan, chief of the Mongols. As the head of a huge empire inherited from his grandfather, Genghiz Khan, Kublai hoped to conquer all of China for his realm. He staged a dress rehearsal at Dali first. When the kingdom fell to the Mongol invaders, most of the Dai population fled west and south, leaving an empty land. Kublai Khan went on to conquer China with the help of tough Muslim mercenaries from Persia and Central Asia. Once established in Beijing, he sent these fierce troops to Yunnan, partly to keep them out of mischief far from the capital, but also to repopulate the southwest. The Muslim settlers also served as the emperor's watchdogs against any movements for independence.

Yunnan became a land of foreigners, Muslim and Mongol. It was the last area of China to hold out when the indigenous Ming Dynasty over-threw the Mongols in 1382, thus inviting another invasion. The Ming emperor's forces drove out or killed all foreign groups brought in by the cosmopolitan Mongols. Only some of the Muslims were allowed to stay. One such Muslim from Yunnan, Zheng He, rose to become the new em-peror's admiral, and a great explorer of the world (see page 81). Ming viceroys in Yunnan built an extensive canal system, added a massive city wall to Yunnanfu (Kunming) and constructed Chinese-style temples.

For centuries, the Ming Dynasty, and the Qing (Manchu) Dynasty that followed it, ruled Yunnan as a colony rather than as a true province of China. It served China as a kind of Siberia, a place of exile for criminals, dissidents, and officials who fell out of favour with the emperor. The actual number of progressive thinkers and intellectuals banished there was relatively small but they brought with them the language, architecture and customs of north China. One lasting sign of their influence is the style of Kunming's roofs, reminiscent of the imperial splendour in Beijing.

In the 18th century, the Qing emperor used Yunnan as a springboard for launching successful military expeditions against the Burmese. Thereafter, 'tribute elephants' carrying jade from Upper Burma and rubies from Mandalay plodded along the old Burma Road to Yunnanfu. There the tribute was transferred to pack horses and sent north to Beijing. Yunnan was still treated as a semi-barbaric colony, only fit for exiles, but along its borders big changes were taking place. Burma soon fell under the influence of the ever-growing British Empire, and the French established themselves in Tonkin, their first step into Indochina. Both European empires eyed Yunnan's rich tin and copper mines covetously.

In 1855, a dispute between Muslim and Chinese miners escalated into a full-scale Muslim rebellion against Chinese rule. It raged on for almost 20 years. Muslims ransacked Kunming's old temples, burned its monasteries, destroyed Buddhist monuments (except for two pagodas), and levelled most public buildings and large private homes. They set up their own capital in Dali. The European powers were quick to take advantage of the chaos in Yunnan. Britain supplied arms to the Muslims through Burma, while France sent arms to the emperor.

Chinese troops finally crushed the rebellion with great cruelty in 1873, slaughtering every Muslim man, woman and child in Dali and sweeping on to massacre thousands more in smaller towns. Plague broke out, killing many of the survivors. Yunnan was nearly depopulated for the second time in its turbulent history. France and Britain both wangled concessions from the failing Qing Dynasty — the French to build a railway into Yunnan from their new colonial capital in Hanoi, and the British to open trade. In 1911 China became a republic and Yunnan fell into the hands of local warlords.

Japan's invasion of China in 1937 heralded World War II and inflicted immense damage. Nonetheless, it brought modernization and progress to Yunnan. Factories, universities and government agencies were evacuated there when the Japanese occupied China's east coast. Fresh population, new ideas and money poured in. Industries were set up. The Burma Road funnelled supplies into Yunnan, destined for Allied war bases all over China. Strategically placed Kunming became a major American base, host to General Chenault's Flying Tigers and General Stilwell's land troops.

The war convinced Yunnan's population that its best interests lay with China. In 1949, there was very little resistance to Chairman Mao's liberation forces. Since then, Yunnan has enjoyed more prosperity than at any time in its history. Its mines and natural resources have been developed, and modern transportation has overcome its old curse of remoteness and inaccessibility. Its natural beauty, healthy climate, and the friendliness of its people have combined to make it one of China's most attractive areas. A trip through Yunnan is unlike any other in China, a panorama of ever-changing scenery, a kaleidoscope of colourful costumes, music and folklore.

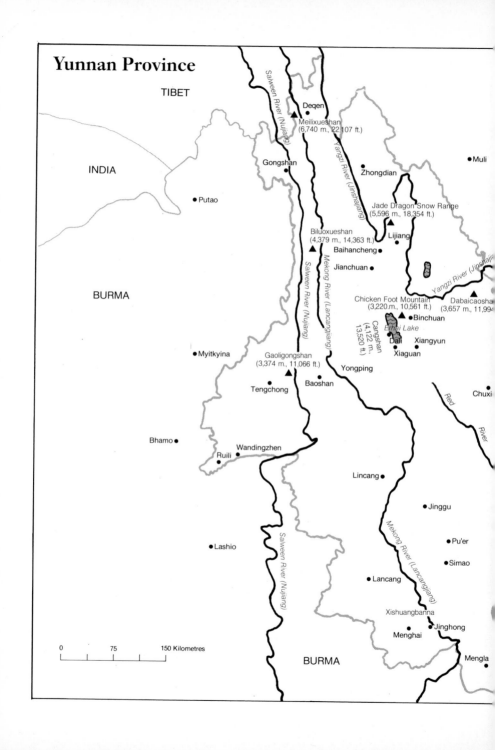

Yunnan Province

TIBET

INDIA

BURMA

Salween River (Nujiang)

Yangzi River (Jinshajiang)

Deqen

Meilixueshan
(6,740 m., 22,107 ft.)

Gongshan

Zhongdian

Muli

Putao

Jade Dragon Snow Range
(5,596 m., 18,354 ft.)

Biluoxueshan
(4,379 m., 14,363 ft.)

Lijiang

Baihancheng

Jianchuan

Mekong River (Lancangjiang)

Salween River (Nujiang)

Yangzi River (Jinshajia

Chicken Foot Mountain
(3,220.m., 10,561 ft.)

Dabaicaosha
(3,657 m., 11,994

Binchuan

Cangshan
(4,122 m.,
13,520 ft.)

Erhai Lake

Dali Xiangyun

Myitkyina

Gaoligongshan
(3,374 m., 11,066 ft.)

Xiaguan

Yongping

Baoshan

Tengchong

Chuxi

Red

Bhamo

Wandingzhen

Ruili

Lincang

River

Jinggu

Lashio

Pu'er

Simao

Mekong River (Lancangjiang)

Lancang

Salween River (Nujiang)

Xishuangbanna

Jinghong

Menghai

0   75   150 Kilometres

BURMA

Mengla

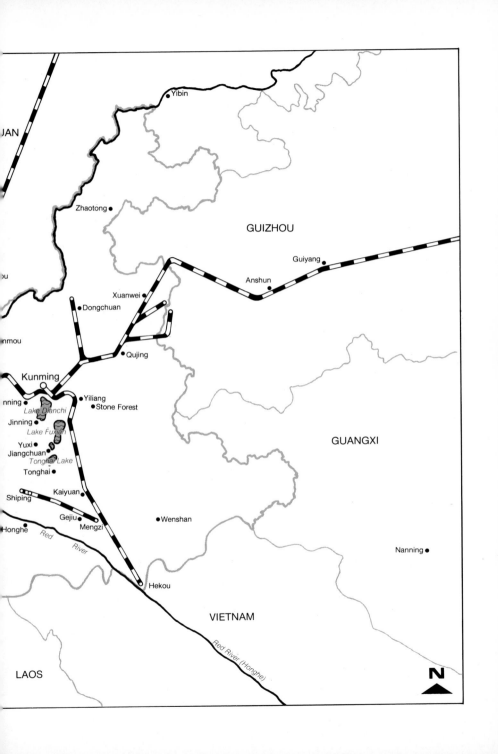

Getting to Yunnan

In the early part of the 20th century, Yunnan was almost inaccessible to foreigners. The arduous, overland trip up the Yangzi River to Chongqing (Chungking) and south through brigand-infested mountains to Kunming was considered too dangerous. Most travellers chose to take the sea route from Hong Kong to Haiphong, in Vietnam, and the French-run railway from Hanoi to Kunming (see page 91).

Yunnan is tucked into China's southwest corner. It is bounded on the south by Vietnam and Laos, and on the west by Burma. Although it is now reached easily by air or train, a trip there still carries the cachet of remoteness and true adventure.

By air

The commonest, quickest way for travellers to reach Kunming, Yunnan's capital, is by air from Hong Kong.

Flights between Hong Kong and Kunming by China's national carrier, CAAC (Civil Aviation Administration of China), take two hours and leave every Tuesday and Saturday. Dragonair, Hong Kong's new airline, flies to Kunming every Wednesday and Sunday. For tourists already inside China, there are daily flights to Kunming from Beijing, Shanghai and Guangzhou. Flights from Xi'an go five times a week, and from Guilin three times.

A CAAC flight every Wednesday links Kunming and Bangkok. It leaves Kunming in the morning and returns from Bangkok in the afternoon.

One of the world's more recherché flights is the link between Burma's capital, Rangoon, and Kunming. CAAC runs the round trip, Kunming-Rangoon-Kunming, on alternate Wednesdays.

By train

The engineering feat of linking Yunnan by rail to the rest of China was tremendous, only accomplished in the 1960s and early 1970s. Mountains, ravines and landslides were overcome. Now that trains are safe and comfortable, the railway is a spectacular way to enter Yunnan.

There are three classes of accommodation on all long-distance trains, known as 'soft sleeper' (first class), 'hard sleeper' (second class) and 'hard seat' (third class). Groups travelling under the care of CITS (China International Travel Service) ride first class; this provides clean, comfortable European-style compartments with four soft berths, a potted plant, lace curtains and porcelain teacups, which all add a quaint charm. Bedding is provided and each carriage has an adequate washing room with hot water and a western-style toilet.

Second class, favoured by most budget travellers, provides six berths, three on each side, in a bay opening on the corridor. The middle of the three berths is the best; the bottom berth is used as a seat by all occupants during the day. Bedding is provided and there are overcrowded washing facilities with an Asian-style toilet. Second-class travel offers the chance to be a part of Chinese life, where food, companionship and conversation are freely shared, without much discomfort.

Third class is cheap, crowded and uncomfortable. Benches facing each other across a small table are built to seat three adults but frequently hold whole families and their possessions, which overflow into the aisle. Washing facilities and toilets are unmentionable. Most Chinese travel third class.

Guangzhou (Canton)-Kunming This daily train leaves Guangzhou's station at 11.35 pm and takes 55 hours. It involves a change of train at Hengyang in Hunan Province. The trip gives an intimate view of the entire breadth of south China, including the fantastic karst mountains made famous by China's classical landscape painters.

Beijing-Kunming This daily express departs Beijing at 11.59 pm and takes approximately 60 hours, crossing China diagonally through a great variety of provinces and terrain.

Chengdu-Kunming This daily train takes about 24 hours. It leaves Chengdu at 4.15 pm and traverses one of the most astounding rail lines in the world. Over 400 tunnels pierce the mountains while over 600 bridges span dizzying gorges. Remote stations often afford a glimpse of shy and rarely seen minorities from the surrounding mountain fastness.

General Information for Travellers

Visas

Everyone must get a visa to go to China, but this is usually an easy, trouble-free process. Tourists travelling in a group are listed on a single group visa — a special document listing all members of the group which is issued in advance to tour organizers. Individual passports of people travelling on a group visa will not be stamped unless specifically requested.

Tourist visas for individual travellers (those who are not travelling in a group) can be obtained directly through Chinese embassies and consulates, although some embassies are more enthusiastic about issuing them than others. Certain travel agents and tour operators around the world can arrange individual visas for their clients. It is simplest in Hong Kong, where there are a large number of travel agents handling visa applications. Just one passport photograph and a completed application form are necessary. The need for exit visas for foreigners leaving China was dropped in 1986.

Visa fees vary considerably, depending on the source of the visa, and on the time taken to get it. In Hong Kong, for instance, some travel agents can get you a tourist visa in a few hours, but it may cost around US$30, while a visa which takes 48 hours to obtain might cost just US$9.

The visa gives you automatic entry to all China's open cities and areas (there were 436 in 1987). Travel permits to certain areas of China, which used to be needed in addition to the visa, were dropped in 1986.

Regular business visitors are eligible for a multiple re-entry visa which may be obtained with the help of a business contact in China. Some Hong Kong travel agents can also arrange re-entry visas for clients — the cost might be around US$50−60.

Single-entry tourist visas are generally for a period of 90 days, but can be extended once you are in China.

Climate and Clothing

Yunnan has the best climate in China. Kunming is known throughout the country as 'Spring City'. Temperatures there rarely reach freezing in winter, and the days are crisp and sunny. The rainy season lasts from late May through August but on most days there is sunshine between the showers. Spring and autumn are sublime. The high altitude causes some fluctuations of temperature, and nights are generally chilly.

Clothing should be simple and consist of layers which can be added or removed as temperatures vary during a day. A sweater and windbreaker will be useful and stout, comfortable shoes are recommended. Special items to bring to Yunnan include sunscreen lotion and sun glasses against the intense sunlight, and a hat. The high, dry plateau is likely to cause chapped lips and cracked skin; lip salve and skin cream should not be forgotten.

Travel to the southern part of Yunnan Province requires light, cotton clothing suitable for the tropics. Travellers to Dali or Lijiang in the northwest of the province should take gloves and a warm coat or jacket between October and March.

Transportation

Yunnan's provincial rail system is limited due to the mountainous terrain.

By bus Buses are by far the commonest form of transport within Yunnan Province. Although buses are old and rickety, the system is remarkably extensive and reliable. Kunming is the hub of the system. The main bus station for all long-distance travel within the province is the Passenger Transport Bus Station (Qiche Keyun Zhan) near the Railway Station, at the southern end of Beijing Lu. Other departure points are West Station (Xi Zhan) and East Station (Dong Zhan), and Xiao Xi Men Station (see map on page 34).

CITS For travellers in groups, China International Travel Service (CITS) automatically provides a vehicle as part of the package arrangement. CITS has a big fleet of modern buses, minibuses, sedans and jeeps. It controls a taxi fleet as well and these vehicles can be hired for both short and long-distance trips. In and around Kunming the fixed rate is Rmb0.80 per kilometre (Rmb1.1 per mile). On longer trips, such as to the Stone Forest or Dali, the rate is Rmb1.50 per kilometre. Every vehicle has its own driver, who does not expect a tip.

Taxis Taxis are on call at Kunming's two main hotels. The taxi stand at the Green Lake Hotel can be reached at tel. 22192 ext. 352; taxis at the Kunming Hotel at tel. 25011. Private taxi companies also exist in Kunming. They have vehicles of various sorts and vintages which can be hired more cheaply than those of CITS (see Useful Addresses on page 197). Foreigners are not allowed to drive.

Money

Chinese Currency The Chinese currency, which is sometimes referred to as Renminbi or Rmb, meaning 'people's currency', is denominated in *yuan* which are each divided into 10 *jiao*, colloquially called *mao. Jiao* are, in turn, each divided into 10 *fen*. There are large notes for 10, 5, 2 and 1 *yuan*, small notes for 5, 2 and 1 *jiao*, and coins for 5, 2 and 1 *fen*.

Currency Certificates Foreign Exchange Certificates (FEC) were introduced into China in May 1980. They were designed to be used instead of Rmb by foreigners, Overseas Chinese and Chinese from Hong Kong and Macao only, for payments in hotels, Friendship Stores, at trade fairs, and for airline tickets, international phone calls, parcel post etc. In practice, however, FEC quickly became a sought-after form of payment anywhere, and a black market developed between Rmb and FEC. In September 1986 it was announced that FECs were to be phased out in the near future. Shortly afterwards a postponement was announced, so the fate of FEC remained unclear. FEC can be reconverted into foreign currency when you leave China, or they may be taken with you, but it is impossible to change them abroad.

Foreign Currency There is no limit to the amount of foreign currency you can bring into China. It is advisable to keep your exchange vouchers as the bank may demand to see them when you convert Chinese currency back into foreign currency on leaving China.

All the major freely negotiable currencies can be exchanged at the branches of the Bank of China, in hotels and stores. The rates of exchange fluctuate with the international money market.

Cheques and Credit Cards All the usual American, European and Japanese travellers cheques are acceptable. Credit cards are accepted in a limited number of Friendship Stores, hotels and banks. You should check with your credit card company or bank before you rely on this form of payment for your purchases. Personal cheques are sometimes taken in return for goods which are shipped after the cheque is cleared.

Tipping Tipping is forbidden in China.

Holidays

In contrast to the long calendar of traditional Chinese festivals, modern China now has only three official holidays: May Day, 1 October, marking the founding of the People's Republic of China, and Chinese New Year, usually called the Spring Festival in China itself, which comes at the lunar new year.

Communications

Mail in Kunming, incoming and outgoing, is reliable and quite fast if sent by airmail. Telegrams can be sent from post offices. The international telephone service is getting steadily better. Calls can be placed most easily at the communications desks in Kunming's two tourist hotels, where telex service is also available.

Customs Regulations

Upon entering China, all foreigners are required to register watches, radios, cameras, jewellery, typewriters etc. and foreign currency. These must all be accounted for upon leaving the country.

Art objects and antiques obtained in China are closely scrutinized. Antiques should carry a seal showing that they were bought in an official shop. Contemporary art objects should be accompanied by a receipt. Souvenirs bought on the street are usually allowed to pass, but customs officials have been known to confiscate jewellery or curios if they consider that a tourist has purchased 'too much'.

Language

Mandarin (*putonghua*) is China's official language, spoken by more than 700 million people. It is the most widely spoken language in the world. Although technically within the Mandarin-speaking region, Yunnan has its own colourful dialect which outsiders find difficult to understand. Most people understand standard Mandarin, and even a small vocabulary will make your trip more enjoyable (see A Guide to Pronouncing Chinese Names on page 188).

CITS

China International Travel Service, also known as Luxingshe, is responsible for looking after foreign tourists in China (see Useful Addresses on page 197). CITS offers a comprehensive service covering visas, accommodation, transport, food and sight-seeing. It generally deals with group tours but can usually handle individual tourists too. This depends on available resources. Individuals requesting transport, a guide, or other services during peak tourist months of summer and autumn may be disappointed. With sufficient advance notice, CITS is always accommodating.

The Kunming branch of CITS has a high reputation within the travel industry for its efficiency and courtesy. Guides can be provided who speak English, French, German or Japanese. Although the ability and experience of the guides may vary, they are enthusiastic and well above the national average.

Food and Drink

Yunnan cuisine, though not yet well known in the west, is one of the best regional eating experiences in China. Many dishes borrow hot, spicy flavours from neighbouring Sichuan. Others, influenced by periodic migrations from provinces such as Jiangsu, Zhejiang and Guangdong, reflect the subtle, rounded taste of eastern Chinese cuisine. The year-round availability and variety of vegetables provide a seemingly limitless menu.

Specialities found nowhere else include *Xuanwei huotui*, a strong, tasty, country-cured ham. Unlike the rest of China, the Yunnanese appreciate certain dairy products. An excellent mild white cheese (*rubing*) is always eaten fried or steamed in combination with ham or vegetables, especially the tender, emerald-green 'horse' beans (*candou*). In spring and summer eels, caught in the wet rice fields, are a great delicacy and are considered by the Chinese to be among the most nutritious of foods. In Yunnan eel is usually cooked in a rich brown sauce with mild garlic and fresh mint. Many varieties of freshwater fish are available, the champion of which is the big-headed fish (*datouyu*). Pork is the most widely eaten meat, but because of the province's large Muslim population, beef and mutton are readily found. True carnivores interested in a rare experience might want to try the Sheep and Goat Banquet, which includes some 40 ovine dishes.

Mushrooms appear in great profusion when the rains let up in August. The most highly prized of the dozens of varieties are 'chicken-taste mushroom' (*jizong*) and morel, called 'sheep-stomach mushroom' (*yangduxun*). For vegetable lovers, Yunnan is a joy. Lotus root, bamboo shoots, tender young pea-sprouts, Chinese broccoli, 'horse' beans, green garlic shoots, just to mention a few, feature in delectable dishes.

Uniquely Yunnanese is the ceramic steam pot, a squat, round lidded vessel with an internal spout that allows steam to enter and circulate but not escape. Chicken cooked by this technique produces a superior soup entirely from steam and natural juices. This dish, called Steam Pot Chicken (*qiguoji*) comes first on the list of Yunnan's specialities. A remarkable feature, which should not put anybody off, is the inclusion of natural medicinal ingredients used by the Chinese both to enhance flavour and to promote health. These might include ginseng, herbs or dried Himalayan caterpillars.

Another regional favourite is the hot pot (*huoguo*), which is prepared quite differently from its Europeanized version, the *fondue chinoise*. In Yunnan, the copper pot, encircling a charcoal-fuelled chimney, was first introduced by Kublai Khan's conquering Mongol army in the 13th century and is probably the authentic, original version. The pot comes to the table already filled with a dozen ingredients simmering in broth — half a dozen vegetables plus miniature meat balls, tiny stuffed omelettes, beancurd in different forms, transparent noodles and more. Only after the pot is half empty do the diners begin to cook fresh, raw ingredients in the broth. This meal is only eaten in winter and it is a marvellously convivial way to spend a cold evening.

Crossing-the-Bridge Rice Noodles (*guoqiao mixian*) is a dish immortalized by a quaint medieval story from southern Yunnan. A scholar, preparing for the imperial examinations, isolated himself on an island in a lake. His devoted wife was dismayed that the meals she carried to him across a long, wooden bridge always grew cold. But by chance, she discovered the way to keep soup boiling hot was to top it with a thin layer of vegetable oil which prevented the heat from escaping. She was then able to cook the meat and vegetables on the spot without a stove. Of course, her husband passed the exams. Today, by the same technique, diners are presented with a large bowl of scalding broth made from chicken, duck and spareribs, topped by a thin layer of vegetable oil. Numerous side dishes include wafer-thin slices of chicken, liver, fish and pork, green onions, pea-sprouts, Chinese spinach and other seasonal vegetables. Rice noodles, made from rice flour, complete the array. All are quickly put into the broth where, in one bowl, they cook to perfection. This is a light, delicate and highly satisfying meal. The vital element in the success of Crossing-the-Bridge Rice Noodles is the temperature and quality of the broth.

Yunnan is one of China's foremost tea-producing regions and tea is drunk by everybody, usually brewed directly in a large cup with a lid, rather than in a teapot. Green tea of many sorts is the most commonly preferred, though excellent black tea is also available in most hotels.

For beer drinkers, Kunming's own brewery produces the good White Dragon Pool brand (*Bailongtan*), which is somewhat cheaper than China's well-known Qingdao (Tsingtao) beer, exported world-wide from Shandong Province.

Chinese grape wines, mostly from north China, were once notoriously sweet and syrupy. Recently, the French have helped improve Chinese wine making and the results are quite palatable. Rice wines differ from Japanese *sake* in taste, colour and texture, being generally nuttier, darker and thicker. They are served warm in winter. The Chinese call these wines *huang jiu* (yellow wine) or Shaoxing *jiu*, whether or not they really originate from the town of Shaoxing in Zhejiang Province.

Strong spirits are usually drunk only by men, especially at banquets and festive occasions. The Chinese call clear, distilled liquor 'white wine' (*bai jiu*), which should never be confused with white grape wine (*bai putao jiu*). Beware, for *bai jiu* is white lightning! The best known brand is Maotai, but most Chinese actually prefer Wuliangye, a spirit made from five different grains. The latter is always a most acceptable gift, and will bring kudos if offered at a banquet.

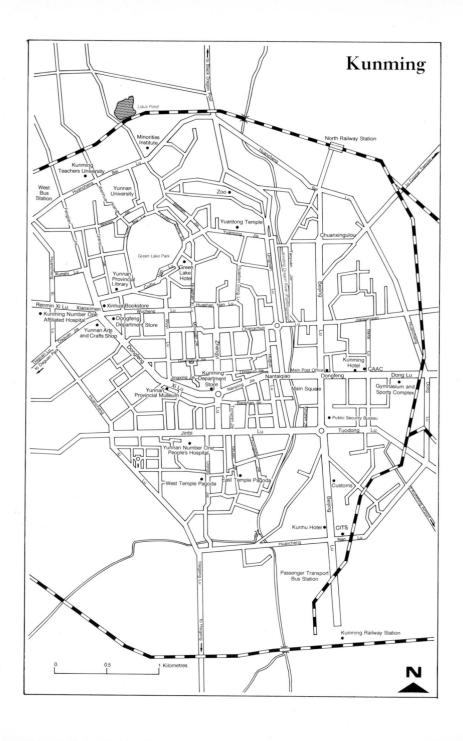

Kunming

Lotus Pond

Minorities
Institute

North Railway Station

Kunming
Teachers University

West
Bus
Station

Yunnan
University

Zoo

Yuantong Temple

Chuanxingulou

Green Lake Park

Yunnan
Provincial
Library

Green
Lake
Hotel

Renmin Xi Lu   Xiaoximen   Xinhua Bookstore
Kunming Number One
Affiliated Hospital
Yunnan Arts
and Crafts Shop

Wucheng
Dongfeng
Department Store

Huashan Nan Lu

Changchun

Kunming
Hotel
CAAC

Dong Lu

to Daguan Park

Dongfeng

Kunming
Department
Store
Jingxing Jie
Yunnan
Provincial Museum

Xi Lu

Nanping
Jie

Nantaiqiao

Main Post Office

Dongfeng

Main Square

Gymnasium and
Sports Complex

Baoshan Jie

Public Security Bureau

Jinbi

Lu

Tuodong   Lu

Yunnan Number One
People's Hospital

West Temple Pagoda   East Temple Pagoda

Customs

Beijing

Kunhu Hotel   CITS
Nan Lu

Huancheng

Passenger Transport
Bus Station

Kunming Railway Station

0.   0.5   1 Kilometres

N

Kunming

Hotels in Kunming

Kunming has two main hotels, both run by CITS. Neither of them match the new, opulent, international-style hotels of Beijing and Guangzhou (Canton) but they are perfectly satisfactory. Several smaller hotels also exist and they too will be listed below for budget travellers or people who want to try something different.

Green Lake Hotel
(Cuihu Binguan)
6 Cuihu Nan Lu
tel. 22192 ext.200
tx. 64027

翠湖宾馆
翠湖南路 6 号

Deluxe suite Rmb250, special suite Rmb80, standard double Rmb72, dormitory Rmb8—10

The Green Lake, Kunming's closest approximation to a first-class hotel, was completely renovated and modernized in the early 1980s. Its 172 rooms all have carpeting, air-conditioning and television. There are four deluxe suites and 20 special suites; these need to be reserved well in advance of arrival. The hotel has a post and telecommunications office, a bank and a one-day film development service. The second floor holds a shopping arcade that carries a good selection of Chinese souvenirs and local arts and crafts (see Shopping on page 42). There is also an excellent restaurant (see Recommended Restaurants on page 38). A bar and coffee shop, popular with young Chinese and foreign residents of Kunming, is on the third floor. On the top floor, a lounge/bar has a terrace overlooking Green Lake Park. Plans for the future include a sauna, a conference centre and a ball room. The Green Lake Hotel is the best place to stay if you can get in.

Kunming Hotel
(Kunming Fandian)
145 Dongfeng
Dong Lu
tel. 23918, 22063
ext. 2111, tx. 64027

昆明饭店
东风东路145号

Suite Rmb80, standard double Rmb70, dormitory Rmb8—10

The 15-storey Kunming Hotel is the major landmark on Kunming's skyline. It is large, with 342 rooms, and somewhat impersonal. Each floor has two suites which are the best rooms in the hotel. Most rooms are standard doubles with private, western-style bathrooms. In addition, there are second-class doubles where four persons share one bathroom. The capacious dormitory on the 14th floor is famous among young travellers as a gathering place and information-swapping centre. There are also dormitory rooms in the old, four-storey building adjacent to the new Kunming Hotel.

The hotel has an abundance of restaurants. Groups eat on the second floor and individuals on the ground floor. Chinese and western food is available and banquets can be arranged for about Rmb25 per person. Various services such as post office, bank and shops are found in the great marble hall on the ground floor. A ticket booking office is also located in the main hall, though CITS headquarters is in the southern part of the city, on Huancheng Nan Lu.

West Garden Hotel
(Xi Yuan Fandian)
Kunming Xi Jiao
tel. 29969

西园饭店
昆明西郊

This villa-style hotel is located in spacious grounds in one of Kunming's western suburbs at the foot of the majestic Western Hill. This was formerly the country retreat of a warlord. The buildings and gardens are built on the French colonial model on the edge of Lake Dianchi. In the main villa there are ten double rooms with bath. The outer buildings contain 20 dormitory rooms with communal washing facilities. Meals are served at the villa. Two launches for visitors make excursions on the lake with simple meals aboard. Transportation to downtown Kunming is by CITS taxi or public bus on the main road.

Kunhu Hotel
(Kunhu Fandian)
Beijing Lu

昆湖饭店
北京路

This simple hotel is conveniently located near Kunming's main bus and railway stations in the southern part of the city. It is a better than average Chinese inn, but below standard for fastidious foreigners. Most rooms have four beds, and everyone shares the bathroom at the end of the hall. The atmosphere is friendly and standard Chinese fare is served in the dining room.

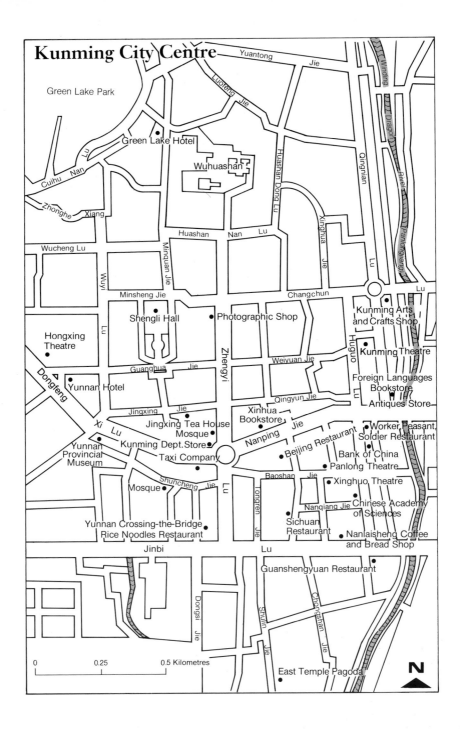

Recommended Restaurants in Kunming

Kunming's numerous restaurants range in quality from excellent to dreadful, and in taste from Cantonese to Sichuanese. But above all, visitors should eat a first-class Yunnanese meal. Listed below is a sampling of Kunming's best known eating spots. CITS can help you plan a menu and reserve a private dining room. If you are courageous and want local colour, take your luck amidst the wedding parties, student celebrations and groups of common folk who make up a restaurant's normal clientele. Restaurants in Kunming close early; you should plan to sit down for dinner before 7 pm.

Green Lake Hotel Restaurants
(Cuihu Binguan Fandian)
6 Cuihu Nan Lu
tel. 22192 ext. 238

翠湖宾馆饭店
翠湖南路 6 号

The Green Lake Hotel is well known for its good cooking. A small army of over 80 chefs, four of them of the highest rank, can turn out a widely variegated menu and cater for large or small groups. They specialize in all of Yunnan's most famous dishes and are renowned for the dazzling presentation of food for festive occasions. Full banquets should be discussed with the chefs and cost between Rmb200−800 for eight people. Regular meals are in the area of Rmb15 per person. There are two main dining rooms and two smaller ones.

Kunming Hotel Attached Restaurant
(Kunming Fandian Fushe Canting)
Baita Lu   tel. 22203

昆明饭店附设餐厅
白塔路

This popular restaurant is situated just to the east of the Kunming Hotel. It is under separate management from the hotel and has better cooks. They serve up a big variety of inexpensive dishes such as Crispy-Skin Chicken (*cuipiji*) and a good fish soup. It is noisy and sometimes quite crowded but can offer a welcome change from the standard hotel fare.

Yunnan Crossing-the-Bridge Rice Noodles Restaurant
(Yunnan Guoqiao Mixian Fandian)
Nantong Jie
tel. 22610

云南过桥米线饭店
南通街

This Kunming favourite has been around for more than 50 years, though it is now housed in a new utilitarian building. As the name suggests, the special noodle dish reigns here. Other items are on the menu but any visit to Yunnan must include Crossing-the-Bridge Rice Noodles. This restaurant is almost always full, so plan to come before 6 pm.

Dongfeng Restaurant
(Dongfeng Canting)
Wuyi Lu   tel. 22905

东风餐厅
五一路

Steam Pot Chicken (*qiguoji*) is the speciality here and the high reputation of the restaurant rests on the careful preparation of this delicious dish. The former name of the establishment was Vitality Cultivating Restaurant, a reference to the healthful properties of steam pot chicken.

Beijing Restaurant
(Beijing Fandian)
77 Xinxiangyun Jie
tel. 23214

北京饭店
新祥云街77号

Common and rare dishes from north China provide an alternative to the good food of Yunnan. Familiar dishes include steamed and pan fried dumplings, onion and chicken cakes and Beijing duck. Less familiar are Five-Willow Fish (excellent), Eight-Treasure Chicken (stuffed with delicacies) and sizzling sea cucumbers. There is an extensive menu adroitly cooked by a team of experienced chefs.

Guanshengyuan Guangwei Fandian
(Cantonese Restaurant)
Jinbi Lu
tel. 22970, 25266

冠生园(广味饭店)
金碧路

A fixture of Kunming's eating scene for half a century, this large, two-storey Cantonese-style restaurant is a great favourite among locals for any festive occasion. Its *dim sum* is varied and good and there is a wide choice of pork prepared in different ways. Interesting chicken dishes and seafood dishes, such as abalone with oyster sauce, round out an ample menu.

More restaurants, and coffee shops

Sichuan Restaurant (Chuanwei Fandian)
Xiangyun Jie tel. 23171
Specializing in Sichuan cuisine
四川饭店(川味饭店) 祥云街

Fushunju Restaurant (Fushunju Fandian)
42 Xiaodong Lu tel. 23872
Specializing in Henan cuisine
福顺居 小东路42号

Worker, Peasant, Soldier Restaurant
(Gongnongbing Fandian) 262 Huguo Lu
tel. 25679
Large restaurant with North China and Sichuan cooking
工农兵饭店 护国路262号

Guoweixiang Restaurant Dongjiawan Arcade
Cuihu Bei Lu
Specializing in Yunnan cuisine
果味香餐厅 翠湖北路董家湾商场

Nanlaisheng Coffee and Bread House
(Nanlaisheng Kafei Mianbao Dian) 299 Jinbi Lu
南来盛咖啡面包店 金碧路299号

Jingxing Teahouse (Jingxing Wenyi Chashi)
37 Jingxing Jie
景星文艺茶室 景星街37号

Shopping in Kunming

Compared to the markets of Beijing, Shanghai and Canton, Kunming is
not a great shopping centre. It does have interesting and unusual items
related to the large ethnic minority population, however, and rare animal
and vegetable products deriving from Yunnan's combination of high
altitude and southern latitude.

Kunming is a small enough city that most shopping can be done on
foot. The main shops are listed at the back of the book (see Useful
Addresses on page 197) and marked on the city map (see page 37).

The bright clothing and embroidered accessories of Yunnan's minority
peoples are favourite purchases. Aprons, shoulder bags, embroidered
shoes, head-dresses and belts are particularly attractive. Decorated baby
hats, capes, and beautifully appliquéd *beibeis* (padded cloth baby carrier,
tied to the mother's back) are charming and amusing. Attractive blue and
white batik cloth is made up into handbags, dresses, napkins and table-
cloths. The Minorities Department Store is the source of many such items
as well as cloth, braid, ornaments, buttons and lace. This store also has
musical instruments, shoes and boots, caps and knick-knacks. Shops in the
Green Lake and Kunming Hotels are also a good place to buy minority
items unless you plan to go to the places where the people actually live.

Everyday Chinese clothing of good cotton or silk makes a good buy —
brightly coloured sweat suits, striped T-shirts, corduroy jackets, silk
blouses, dress shirts. These can all be found at the two main department
stores on Dongfeng Lu.

Antique shops in Kunming carry mostly porcelains and the usual miscellaneous assortments of chops, snuff bottles, ink stones and wrought
silver jewellery. Apart from a lucky find, there is nothing very special here.
Some visitors have been impressed by the jade, which comes from neighbouring Burma and from quarries in Yunnan. Marble items from Dali can

be found everywhere, ranging from finely polished discs with landscapes in the natural grain to heavy, crude flower pots. For a further discussion of Dali marble, see page 118.

Yunnan's special cooking utensils, the ceramic steam pot (*qiguo*) and the copper hot pot (*huoguo*) are handsome and versatile. Other copper items for the kitchen include ladles, bowls, moulds and kettles.

Kunming has several bookshops which are good places to browse for light, inexpensive gifts. The Foreign Language Bookshop has interesting books in English, French, German and other languages on Chinese history, learning Chinese, poetry, contemporary life and children's stories. The large Xinhua Bookshop has colourful posters, maps, art and calligraphy books and outstanding calendars.

Many of Yunnan's native products are highly sought after by the Chinese themselves. If you ever need to give a gift or repay a kindness inside China, the following items are thoroughly appropriate. They can also be seen as authentic souvenirs from Southwest China.

Tea Many varieties of local tea exist; some of the best known names are Pu'er, Tuo, Dianlu and Dabaicha. Yunnan black tea is also excellent.

Medicines Chinese from all over the world come to Yunnan for its traditional medicines. Some familiarity with the products is necessary for successful shopping, and the mere reading of the packages sends many foreigners reeling. Chinese angelica, a herb of the carrot family, is favoured as a pain killer, helps blood circulation and is good for the stomach. Pseudo-ginseng (*sanqi* and *tianqi*) is considered an ideal preventive medicine for cardiovascular disease. *Baiyao* is a traditional folk remedy made from over 100 kinds of herbs that can cure bruises, internal haemorrhaging and gunshot wounds. These are just a few of the pharmacopaeia available.

Cigarettes Most Chinese recognise that the best tobacco in the country comes from Yunnan. The prized brands are Yunyan, Red Camellia, Red Pagoda Mountain and Dazhongjiu.

Food and spirits Yunnan ham (*Xuanwei huotui*), either fresh or tinned, is a delicious gift, as are the many types of dried mushrooms. Although not distilled in the province, favourite white liquors are Wuliangye, Maotai and Tequ.

Sights in Kunming

Yunnan Provincial Museum

Some tourists skip museums on principle, but in this case they really
should make an exception. Kunming's museum, housed in a monumental
Russian-style building, holds some truly superb cultural treasures. One of
its main collections consists of costumes, handicrafts and artifacts of
Yunnan's 24 ethnic minority groups (see page 50), and the other contains a
priceless assemblage of three-thousand-year-old bronzes (see page 54).
The museum, at the junction of Dongfeng Xi Lu and Wuyi Lu, is open
from 8.30 am until 5 pm daily except Monday.

The cavernous ground floor has two wings. On the left is a hall for
temporary and travelling art shows. On the right is the permanent collection from Yunnan's minority cultures. There are no English labels in the
entire museum but many of the exhibits speak for themselves. The exhibition of the minorities is held in two rooms. The list below identifies the
different groups and points out the highlights.

(1) The **Dai**, slender saronged inhabitants of border regions abutting
Laos and Burma, are represented by costumes from different localities and
by musical instruments. Their nice jewellery includes bangles and an enormous silver necklace.

(2) The **Zhuang** and **Buyi** come from the mountainous eastern part of
the province.

(3) The **Bai** are a well-educated, brightly clad folk from the Dali
region (see page 99). Examples of fine Dali marble are shown, along with a
diorama of Shibaoshan, Yunnan's richest Buddhist cave centre.

(4) The display of the **Hani** from southern Yunnan shows photographs
of their various branches, as well as some of their magnificent jewellery —
particularly earrings.

(5) The **Achang** from the Burmese border are known for their warlike
swords and daggers.

(6) The **Miao** and **Yao**, two widely dispersed minority groups, display
their batiks and musical instruments including the bizarre *lu sheng*, a bamboo wind instrument with many projecting pipes.

(7) The **Jingpo**, scattered through the far west of the province, have
large, two-handed swords and intricate jewellery looking like silver armour.

(8) The primitive **Wa**, concentrated in remote hills between the
Mekong and Salween Rivers on the Burmese border, accompany their
rituals with drums. A bronze drum is displayed with a photograph of a
cylindrical wooden drum beautifully painted in red, black and brown.

(9) The **Benglong**, with fewer than 15,000 members, live among the
western Dai. Their heavy black fabrics are decorated in red and yellow.

(10) The **Bulang** are closely related to the Wa and Benglong.

(11) The **Yi**, fourth largest of China's minorities, boast some 30 branches. A big section shows many and various examples of their dress.

(12) **Tibetans (Zang)** have resided for centuries in northernmost Yunnan near the Tibetan border.

(13) The **Lisu, Nu** and **Dulong** are people of northwestern Yunnan from extremely isolated areas along the Salween River. Besides their costumes there is a photograph of a Dulong with a tattooed face.

(14) The **Naxi**, a matriarchal people from the Lijiang area (see page 129), are well respresented. A coloured cartoon-like scroll made by *dongbas*, or shamans, depicts deities and infernal creatures. Other rare *dongba* artifacts include ritual trumpets.

(15) The **Pumi** are spread across west and north Yunnan. They are known for their colourful costumes and a rich oral tradition.

(16) The **Lahu** are mountain dwellers, neighbours of the Wa. They are represented here by their simple agricultural implements.

(17) The **Jinuo** number only 12,000 and are the most recent minority to be recognized as such by Chinese anthropologists.

(18) The **Muslims (Hui)**, scattered throughout the province, are considered a minority because of their religion and culture, although physically and linguistically they resemble the majority Han. A photograph shows a handsome mosque, built in Chinese temple style, with colourful geometric panels.

(19) The **Mongolians (Menggu)**, remnants of Kublai Khan's conquering army, number only 4,000 and dwell in self-contained villages near Tonghai, in central Yunnan.

On the upper floor of the museum, two halls are devoted entirely to Yunnan's archaeology, most notably the famous bronzes (see page 54). Four major Bronze-Age sites have been excavated since 1955. Shizhaishan, at the southern tip of Lake Dianchi, and Jiangchuan, 100 kilometres (63 miles) south of Kunming, were at the heart of an ancient kingdom named Dian which flourished from 1200 BC until the first century BC. Chuxiong, 185 kilometres (116 miles), and Xiangyun, 340 kilometres (212 miles) west of Kunming, were home to a western branch of the Dian culture. Their art was less refined and used less decoration than the masterpieces found in tombs at Shizhaishan and Jiangchuan. Dian artisans were among the first people in the world to cast metal by the lost wax method. A clear model of a bronze drum being cast by this method is displayed at the centre of the exhibition.

Long-horned, high-humped cattle played a central role in Dian culture. A measure of wealth, the beasts were only used for sacrifice, never for agriculture. A beautiful use of the ox motif in art can be seen on a bronze sacrificial table. The head, chest and forelegs of the powerful animal form one end; the flat table surface represents its back; its upturned tail and hind quarters are being attacked by an acrobatic tiger. A small-horned calf, appearing crosswise under the table, completes the composition. Function, concept and craftsmanship blend to meet the needs of a sacrificial ceremony. In another display case, an elegant bronze head-rest uses ox heads for its raised points while cattle and horses in light relief decorate its base.

The most intriguing exhibits reveal details of life on the Yunnan plain three thousand years ago. The lids of giant cowrie holders become circular arenas on which figurines play out various vivid scenes. Cowrie holders were essentially treasuries, containing the cowrie shells that served as currency throughout Southeast Asia. (Cowries continued to be used as money in Yunnan until the early 20th century and the shells can still be seen sewn into the head-dresses of minority costumes displayed downstairs.)

The scenes depict hand-to-hand battles, ceremonial tribute-payment, head-hunting expeditions, a slave-owner overseeing women weavers, and all sorts of daily actions that draw you intimately into a distant way of life. Some of the figurines have big, western noses, round eyes, beards and heavy clothing, raising the possibility of early migrations from Central Asia. The details are wonderful and they tell much about the material and philosophical world of the Dian.

One elaborate piece shows an altar at which two slave-owners are consecrating an alliance. To the left and right of the altar, cattle are being slaughtered to strains of music. Tigers and horses are being fed. Behind the altar, a human sacrifice is in progress. Though rich and crowded, the whole configuration is a masterpiece of balanced symmetry.

Bronze drums form a whole category of their own. Some are immense in size, beautifully decorated in relief, with stylized frogs as handles. The earliest bronze drum in the world, dating from the sixth century BC, was found in Yunnan. Members of the Wa minority use bronze drums to this day, as do primitive tribes elsewhere in Southeast Asia.

Some of the most impressive objects in the exhibition are small statues of animals. Their meticulous, forceful realism has rarely been surpassed in any age. This author's favourites are a peacock with a snake in its mouth, two tigers attacking a boar, a wild duck catching fish and two bulls in mortal struggle. An ensemble showing a wolf and a leopard fighting over a disembowelled deer is filled with emotion, pathos and awe at the power of nature.

On a lighter note, do not miss the outrageous little *pas-de-deux* performed by two drunkards. Dancing barefoot on a snake, with swords at their sides, they sing and shout while balancing bowls on their palms.

The Minority Nationalities

China is a vast country, slightly larger than the United States in surface area, sharing borders with 11 different nations. Its geographical and human make-up is extremely complex; not the mono-dimensional, grey place stereotyped by many outsiders.

The Han Chinese (the name Han comes from China's first long-lasting, unified empire, 206 BC−AD 220) are by far the most important nationality in the country, comprising 94 per cent of the population, but 55 other nationalities, the 'minorities', occupy over 60 per cent of the land mass, much of it in strategic border areas. The Chinese have always realized the significance of these people, who from time to time through the centuries have made their presence known with a vengeance. Barbarian nomads in the north, indefatigable Tibetans in the west and a host of lesser nations on the periphery have chipped away at China whenever it showed vulnerability. Two great dynasties, the Yuan (Mongol) and Qing (Manchu), proved the ascendency of non-Chinese peoples at critical moments in history.

Yunnan is a microcosm of China in the areas of minority affairs and nationality relations. The province has 24 minority groups, nearly half of the country's total. With such ethnic diversity it is important to ask the question: what criteria are used to determine minority status and classification? Basically, there are five ways.

1. Race
2. Language
3. Culture
4. Religion
5. History

In Yunnan race is not a major consideration, as it is in northwest China where Caucasian minorities exist. Language and culture, however, are of primary interest because they are the basis for classifying most minority nationalities. Religion plays a role in groups such as the Hui (Muslims) who, for all intents and purposes, are Chinese except for their faith. Historical background can sometimes tip the balance in determining the status of a people. The Bai, who have a high cultural level and speak a language closely related to Mandarin, are clearly not Chinese on the basis of their long, well-recorded and independent history.

The linguistic situation in China is very complicated and becomes even more so in Yunnan. Although 700 million Chinese speak Mandarin, the national language, and many more speak well-known secondary languages, such as Cantonese and Shanghainese, the babel of minority tongues is impressive and daunting.

Five major language groups exist in China: Sino-Tibetan, Altaic,

Austroasiatic, Indo-European and Austronesian. Three appear in Yunnan, represented by many smaller language families, of which our knowledge is still incomplete. Some are scarcely known at all and most have not been sufficiently recorded; a main reason for this lacuna was the absence of writing among most minority nationalities. While certain groups did have writing, such as the Bai with their use of Chinese characters, the Hui (Muslims) with their Arabic script, the Naxi with their arcane *dongba* pictographs and the Tibetans with their syllabary borrowed from India, most needed the help of missionaries or contemporary linguists to create a written language.

To the casual observer, the panoply of minority peoples, their peculiar, unfamiliar names, dazzling costumes and wild festivals become little more than an exotic blur. It takes time and effort to differentiate between the groups, to appreciate at a deeper level their special life and unique place among the cultures of the world.

Here is a list of Yunnan Province's 24 minority nationalities. A map showing their geographical distribution is on page 52.

Name	Population	Language Family
Yi	3,000,000	Tibeto-Burman
Bai	1,050,000	Tibeto-Burman
Hani	930,000	Tibeto-Burman
Zhuang	840,000	Tai
Dai	770,000	Tai
Miao	650,000	Miao-Yao
Hui (Muslim)	400,000	Sinitic
Lisu	325,000	Tibeto-Burman
Lahu	275,000	Tibeto-Burman
Wa	270,000	Mon-Khmer
Naxi	250,000	Tibeto-Burman
Yao	140,000	Miao-Yao
Zang (Tibetan)	90,000	Tibeto-Burman
Jingpo	85,000	Tibeto-Burman
Bulang	55,000	Mon-Khmer
Pumi	22,000	Tai
Achang	20,000	Tibeto-Burman
Nu	20,000	Tibeto-Burman
Jinuo	12,000	Tibeto-Burman
Benglong	10,000	Mon-Khmer
Menggu (Mongolian)	4,000	Mongol
Dulong	4,000	Tibeto-Burman

In addition, small numbers of Buyi live within Yunnan's eastern borders. The Kucong, not formally recognized as a minority nationality, live in southern Yunnan near the Vietnamese border and form the 24th distinct ethnic group.

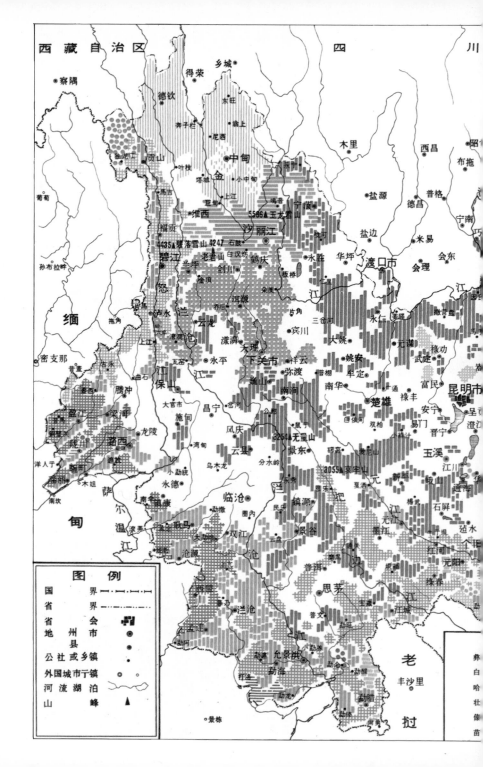

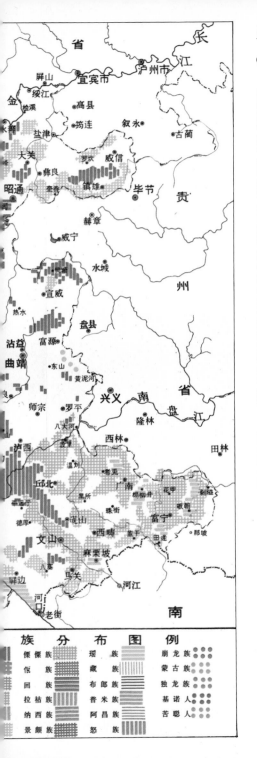

Minority Nationalities of Yunnan Province

▥	Yi
▦	Bai
▦	Hani
▦	Zhuang
▥	Dai
▥	Miao
▤	Hui (Muslim)
▦	Lisu
▥	Lahu
▦	Wa
▤	Naxi
▬	Yao
▥	Zang (Tibetan)
▦	Jingpo
▤	Bulang
▤	Pumi
▤	Achang
▥	Nu
⠿	Jinuo
⠿	Benglong
⠿	Menggu (Mongolian)
⠿	Dulong
⠿	Kucong
⠿	Buyi

The Bronzes of Yunnan

The discovery in Yunnan of magnificent bronze artwork from the dawn of history excited archaeologists around the world. Farmers ploughing near Lake Dianchi unearthed some mystifying bronze vessels in the early 1950s and notified the provincial museum in Kunming. In 1955, archaeologists struck a treasure trove of 48 Bronze-Age tombs at Stone Village Hill (Shizhaishan), 40 kilometres (25 miles) south of Kunming.

Bronze is an alloy of copper and tin which is stronger than iron if made in correct proportions — eight parts copper to one part tin. Bronze was the first metal ever used by humans. It first came into use in northern China during the Shang Dynasty, around 1800 BC. Yunnan's bronze culture dates from about 1200 BC, near the end of the Shang Dynasty.

The tombs at Shizhaishan yielded thousands of bronze objects — sewing boxes, figurines, head-rests, mirrors, weapons, farm implements, belt buckles and more. Animals, hunting and fighting, took a predominant place among the statuettes and decorations. Archaeologists found 34 recognizable species along with many mythological beasts. Subsequent digs in western Yunnan produced a little bronze house with six kinds of domesticated animals attached — cow, goat, chicken, dog, pig and horse — pointing to an advanced agricultural society.

Even more revealing were elaborate, three-dimensional scenes cast on the lids of huge cowrie containers and on drums, showing the daily life of a vigorous, productive, slave-owning people. To archaeologists, this was a unique moment in the history of bronzeware. Only in Yunnan did Bronze-Age artisans realistically record the intimate and unmistakable details of their social activity. There were ferocious miniature battles and lively domestic scenes showing the work of women. The rhythms and rituals of agriculture and religion came to life, along with grisly depictions of head-hunting and human sacrifice. The bronze figurines laughed, wept, got drunk. One scene showed pompously dressed chieftains, surrounded by slaves, offering tribute to the King of Dian. Who were these people?

The first historical reference to the Kingdom of Dian appears in the second century BC. Sima Qian (145−85 BC), China's greatest classical historian, mentions that the King of Dian, in the savage southern border region beyond China, allied himself with the emperor of the Han Dynasty in order to subdue neighbouring tribes. In recognition of Dian's new tributary status, a seal was presented to the King of Dian. Other references to Dian appeared here and there in ancient Chinese literature but there was no hard evidence to confirm the kingdom's existence until 1956. That year, Tomb Number 6 at Shizhaishan yielded up the seal itself. Four clear characters on its bronze face — *Dian Wang Zhi Yin* (Seal of the King of Dian) — bound this remote, remarkable tribe into the vast empire of China.

Dian originally referred only to the mysterious, non-Chinese tribe. Later the name came to mean the territorial kingdom as well. The Lake of Dian (Dianchi) has kept its ancestral name for three millennia and the name Dian remains synonymous with Yunnan.

Yuantong Temple (Yuantongsi), Park and Zoo

The well-restored, thousand-year-old Buddhist temple lies in the north part of the city at the foot of Yuantong Hill. Its elaborate entrance on Yuantong Jie is a short walk from the north terminus of the Number 4 bus route.

The temple was founded in the eighth century, when Yunnan was an independent kingdom adjacent to Tang-Dynasty China. The whole complex was greatly enlarged in 1320 after the conquest of southwest China by the Mongol Emperor Kublai Khan. For centuries it remained the largest Buddhist monastery in Kunming. Today, Yuantong Temple consists of a Great Hall of the Buddha, the Octagonal Pavilion and garden-like walkways around a pond.

Legend says the temple and its monastery were first built to control a malicious dragon who lived in a small pond behind the present buildings. Two huge pillars inside the Great Hall are adorned with carved dragons, reminders of their ancient ancestor.

One of the pleasures of Yuantong Temple is to enjoy a cup of green tea among ornamental plants beside the pond, and breathe in the atmosphere of old China. Centuries-old poems are inscribed on the rocky hillside as you look up towards the park and zoo

Yuantong Park's main entrance lies at the end of Qingnian Lu by the bus terminal. The park, spreading over the slopes of Yuantong Hill, is famous for its flowers and trees. Four main gardens exhibit exquisite blossoms at different times of the year. In summer, many varieties of Yunnan's celebrated rhododendrons are on display. Autumn brings a riot of variegated chrysanthemums. Throughout Kunming's pleasant winter there comes a succession of magnolia, cassia, flowering plum and camellia. The best display of all occurs in late February and March when avenues of Japanese and Oriental cherry create a fairyland of delicate colour.

Kunming's zoo forms the western part of Yuantong Park. Many of Yunnan's indigenous species are found here, including wild oxen, peacocks, elephants, tigers, and the handsome, red, raccoon-like lesser panda — as well as the obligatory giant panda from Sichuan Province. All Chinese zoos are a bit sad but this one is better than most.

East and West Temple Pagodas (Dongsita, Xisita)

South of Jinbi Lu stand two ancient pagodas, the oldest surviving structures in Kunming. As historical and architectural monuments they are invaluable though they may seem run-down at first glance. Both pagodas were constructed in the first half of the ninth century, by a famous artisan named Weichi Chingde.

The 13-tiered pagoda rising 41 metres (135 feet) above Shulin Jie is

known by three different names: East Temple Pagoda, Golden Chicken
Pagoda (the popular name, designating four golden roosters on its summit)
and Changle Temple Pagoda (the scholarly name, denoting a temple that
once surrounded the site). The dilapidated chickens are still there, made of
copper rather than gold. An important Qing-Dynasty stele at its base
describes the history of the two pagodas and their many renovations.

The West Temple Pagoda, also with 13 tiers, is slightly shorter,
squatter, and better preserved than its twin. Unfortunately it stands inside a
private compound off limits to the public, but it can be viewed from Dongsi
Jie.

Green Lake Park (Cuihu Gongyuan)

This lively, attractive park lies in the northwestern quarter of the city. It
can be reached by bus Number 2. Originally a marsh on the outskirts of
Kunming, it was transformed into a park in the late 17th century by
Emperor Kangxi who drained the swamp, put in the lake, built the main
pavilion and installed the causeways and arbours.

In the early morning the park hums with traditional Chinese life:
elderly gentlemen practising martial arts or airing their pet birds, children
exercising, grannies gossiping. The park has recently become a gathering
place for singers who have revived long-dormant folk songs and operas.
Everybody enjoys the spontaneous, open-air performances at any odd time
of day, but most frequently on weekends.

Mosques (Qingzhensi)

At least five mosques serve Kunming's 40,000-strong Muslim population.
The two main ones welcome visitors who behave in a modest and circumspect manner. The oldest and leading mosque of the city is located
adjacent to the Central Department Store at 51 Zhengyi Lu. It is some
400 years old and noted for its murals depicting the holy Islamic sites of
Mecca and Medina.

A larger mosque is situated down a white-washed alley that leaves the
main road at 90 Shuncheng Jie, in the centre of the Muslim quarter of the
city. Quaint shops and halal restaurants specializing in beef and lamb
dishes cater to Muslim tastes in the neighbourhood. The well-preserved
mosque is an interesting mixture of Chinese and Arabic styles. A large
prayer hall with an elaborate roof faces an open courtyard where the white-
clad worshippers come streaming through after daily prayers, especially on
Fridays.

Walking or Bicycling in Town

A walk or a bike ride through Kunming is easy and fun. In spite of a population of one and half million (including the suburbs) it is a compact city, about 4 kilometres (2.5 miles) in diameter, encircled by a ring road, Huancheng Lu. Street names are posted in *pinyin* as well as Chinese characters, so it is easy to follow a map.

A visitor's first impression of the city is often of broad, modern avenues flanked by grey, featureless buildings. A view from the top of the Kunming Hotel will show that such arteries merely form a wide grid placed over the ancient city, and that the spaces between them are filled with crooked lanes, low wooden houses with tiled roofs and carved upper storeys, craftsmen's shops, teahouses, little courtyards and tiny gardens. Though constantly under attack by builders and modernizers, these interstices continue to hum with the life-style and flavour of traditional China.

A Walk from the Kunming Hotel (1½ hours)

At the hotel gate, turn right (west) on Dongfeng Dong Lu, Kunming's main avenue, and walk for two long blocks to the main square. Cross the square diagonally towards the southwest corner. The square itself is full of activity at most times of the day and evening — *taiji quan* (tai ch'i) and martial arts are practised in the morning; kite-flying, domino games and street stalls occupy it in the afternoon; a cross-section of the city promenades through it in the evening. When you reach Winding Dragon River (Panlongjiang) turn left and follow the small lane southward along its bank to Jinbi Lu. Picturesque scribes and fortune-tellers often frequent the riverbank. Jinbi Lu's character comes from its role, in former times, as the commercial centre of Kunming's Vietnamese and Cantonese communities. Tinkers, box-makers, scroll-mounters and artisans are juxtaposed with bakeries, tiny sweet shops and coffee shops. Turn right on Jinbi Lu and walk westward for about five blocks to Tongren Jie. Turn right down this charming arcaded street to its end at Baoshan Jie. Turn right, and continue for about five blocks past a variety of shops and theatres to Huguo Lu, where a left turn will bring you quickly back to Dongfeng Dong Lu. The square is on your right, and the Kunming Hotel is two blocks beyond that.

A Walk from the Green Lake Hotel (1½ hours)

The hotel stands opposite Green Lake Park, which makes an enjoyable excursion in itself, but for a fuller appreciation of Kunming's old charm, you need to strike out into the neighbouring streets and alleys.

Leaving the main gate turn sharp left and follow the small flagstoned street for a few minutes to a gateway on your left guarded by two tumble-down lions. Inside the courtyard is a cluster of curious old temple buildings, now used as a primary school. Continue straight along the flagstoned lane until it rejoins Cuihu Nan Lu, the road which encircles Green Lake Park, and then bear left for about 300 metres (330 yards).

Turn left on Honghua Qiao until it reaches the distinct main street called
Wucheng Lu, ascending a hill to the left. This bustling thoroughfare is an
agglomeration of eccentric shops selling eyeglasses, alarm clocks, wine,
cloth, noodles, office safes and firecrackers, among other things. At the top
of the hill Wucheng Lu ends at Minquan Jie; turn right. Minquan Jie leads
for about half a kilometre (600 yards) through a quiet, old residential area.
The road veers to the right at the bottom of the hill and joins a main
intersection. Straight ahead is an extraordinary, narrow building, and on
the right a huge flight of stone steps — a favourite haunt of naughty school
boys who sometimes shoot down the stairway riding their mothers'
washboards.

From the steps, cross the main thoroughfare, Guanghua Jie, work your
way around a low warehouse and head straight south on a little, arboured
street, where potted plants and bonsai are often on sale. After one block it
reaches Jingxing Jie. To your left is Kunming's most famous teashop,
rarely noticed by tourists, where traditional bards tell stories, with sound
effects, to enraptured audiences of old men in the afternoons and evenings.
After a cup of tea, backtrack along Jingxing Jie to its end at Wuyi Lu. Turn
right and continue straight north until you finally reach Green Lake Park.
Turn right on Cuihu Nan Lu and you will see the hotel ahead.

University Quarter

Four major institutions of higher education lie on Kunming's northwest
edge beyond Green Lake Park. The campuses flank Huancheng Bei Lu
near the Western Station bus depot. Formal arrangements to visit any of
the institutions can be made through CITS. However, you may just want to
stroll through the university quarter and chat with students informally.

Farthest east is the **Yunnan Institute for Nationalities**, easily recognized by its large, conspicuous entrance gate. Known colloquially as the
Minorities Institute, the campus was set up in 1951 as a training school for
political cadres from Yunnan's 24 ethnic groups. Today the institute offers
a broad curriculum to 1,500 students representing all of Yunnan's minority
peoples.

A few steps to the west, straddling Huancheng Bei Lu, is **Yunnan
University**, the largest and most important of the four institutions.
Established privately in 1923 as Eastern Continental University, it had
evolved into a fully-fledged provincial university by the mid 1930s. After
the 1949 revolution, specialized colleges such as agriculture, medicine, and
engineering were split off and established as independent schools. The
remaining faculties of arts and sciences now boast 5,000 of Yunnan's
brightest students. A walk through the tree-lined campus reveals the architectural history of the university, from the old French-style administration
building to the recently added departments of law and economics. Directly
behind Yunnan University lies **Kunming Engineering College**. Its large

campus peters out in the red hills north of Kunming.

Just west of Yunnan University, on Huancheng Bei Lu, lies **Kunming Teachers University**, which vies with Yunnan University in size and status. Its function is to provide high quality teachers for Yunnan Province's educational system. From 1938 to 1946, this site was occupied by the Southwest Associated University, an institution that played a vital role in modern China's social, intellectual and political history. Refugee teachers and students from universities in Beijing and Tianjin fled across China, pulling their libraries in carts, to escape the invading Japanese. They gathered in Kunming, where they kept alive the flame of free learning throughout the war.

Sights near Kunming

Western Hill (Xishan)

The name Western Hill refers to a range of four mountains stretching over 40 kilometres (25 miles) along the western shore of Dianchi Lake. Seen from a distance, its skyline resembles a Sleeping Beauty with long tresses trailing away to the south. It offers the best scenery and some of the finest temples in the entire region. Its highest temple, Dragon Gate, is nearly 2,500 metres (8,200 feet) high.

The bus stop at the base of Western Hill, called Gao Qiao Station, is 26 kilometres (16 miles) from Xiao Xi Men Station in Kunming. Bus Number 6 travels the route regularly. There is also a direct daily bus from the Yunnan Hotel (see map on page 37) departing at 7.30 am, returning from the Dragon Gate summit at 4 pm. Public minibuses run up and down the mountain between Gao Qiao Station and Dragon Gate, a trip of 20 minutes, but most people prefer the exhilarating climb and the sights to be seen at almost every turn. The 6.5-kilometre (4-mile) route from base to top is central Yunnan's most celebrated pilgrim path.

Western Hill offers four major attractions. On the lower and middle slopes are two important Buddhist Temples. On the steep, higher reaches are a Daoist temple, grottoes, and a superb view across the lake and the whole Yunnan plain from the Dragon Gate itself.

From the bus stop at Gao Qiao Station, a walk of 2.5 kilometres (1.5 miles) along the road brings you to **Huating Temple** (Huatingsi), the largest Buddhist complex in Kunming. A grand garden at the entrance includes an ornamental lake surrounded by a wall with three-metre (ten-foot) high white stupas. These small towers, whose shape derives from ancient burial mounds, are the fundamental symbol of Buddhism. Two wrathful giants known as Heng (with mouth closed) and Ha (mouth open) stand at the temple entrance. Coloured with lacquer, they are considered to be among the best representations of these celestial guardians in China. Inside the entrance hall are even larger statues of the Kings of the Four

*The main hall of Huating
Temple holds three enormous
statues of the Buddha.
Huating, the largest temple
complex on Western Hill, was
an important monastery from
the 14th century onward.
Today it houses 20 monks.*

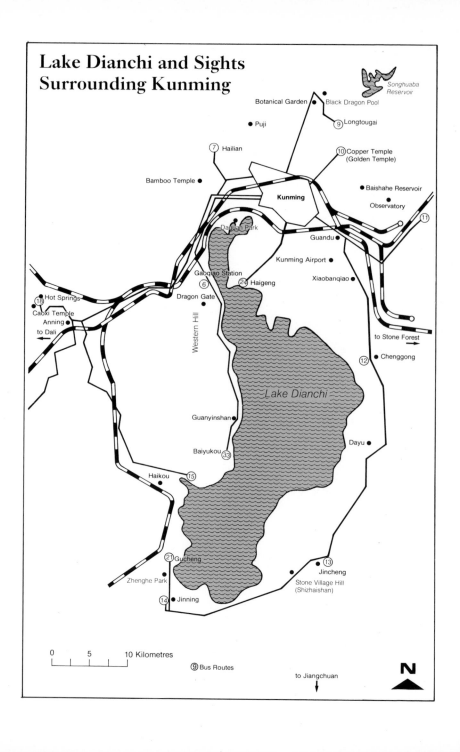

Lake Dianchi and Sights
Surrounding Kunming

Songhuaba Reservoir

Botanical Garden • ● Black Dragon Pool

● Puji (9) Longtougai

(7) Hailian

(10) Copper Temple (Golden Temple)

Bamboo Temple ●

Kunming

● Baishahe Reservoir

Observatory

Daguan Park

(11)

Guandu ●

Kunming Airport ●

Gaoqiao Station

(6) (24) Haigeng

Xiaobanqiao ●

Dragon Gate ●

(18) Hot Springs

Caoxi Temple

Anning ●

to Dali

Western Hill

to Stone Forest

(12) ● Chenggong

Lake Dianchi

Guanyinshan ●

Dayu ●

Baiyukou (33)

Haikou ● (15)

(21) Gucheng

(13)

Jincheng

Zhenghe Park ●

Stone Village Hill
(Shizhaishan)

(14) ● Jinning

0   5   10 Kilometres

(9) Bus Routes

to Jiangchuan

N

Directions, dressed in the splendid armour of Chinese warriors a thousand years ago, before Mongol and Manchu invasions introduced alien martial regalia.

Earliest references to Huating go back to the 11th century. An important monastery in the 14th century, it continued to grow and reached its present dimensions only in 1920. Today, there are 20 monks in residence and newly renovated quarters can accommodate pilgrims and visitors.

The main temple contains a trinity of gilded lacquer Buddhas seated on lotus thrones. Their huge size, blue hair, and sumptuous setting make an impressive sight. The side walls are covered with a phantasmagoria of folk characters — these are the same 500 *luohan* (holy men and disciples of the Buddha) as the ones in the Bamboo Temple (see page 71) — made deliberately comical to contrast with the calm solemnity of the great Buddhas. One, on stilt-like legs, grabs for the moon; another has eyebrows reaching to his knees.

Behind the three Buddhas, facing the back of the hall, is a shrine to Guanyin, the Goddess of Mercy. Against an elaborate backdrop, a kind of mythological bestiary, she rides across the sea on a dragon's head to meet the Dragon King, who waits for her on the left.

Leaving Huating, follow the main road up the mountain for 2 kilometres (1.25 miles) to a secondary road leading sharply off to the right. A short walk brings you to **Taihua Temple** (Taihuasi), which many people feel is aesthetically superior to the larger complex below. Nestled in a deep forest, Taihua's site is one of its charms. Age-old camellia and magnolia trees give shade in a meticulously cultivated garden. The top level at the back offers a stunning view over temple roofs to the lake far below. The mossy, upturned eaves, the ancient, gnarled trees and the square-rigged fishing boats dotting the lake could have emerged straight from a traditional Chinese scroll painting. A visit to this Buddhist retreat in the late afternoon or the cool of the evening, when the crowds have gone, can transport you to another century, far removed from modern China.

At the entrance, a handsome stone archway is covered with fine carvings: Buddhist symbols, flowers and creatures, including a delightfully animated cockatoo. In the Four Guardians entrance hall beyond, an image of Guanyin replaces the usual merry Buddha, as Taihua is dedicated to the Goddess of Mercy.

The main temple building bears the name Hall of the Precious Hero, in honour of a statue near the back representing Zishi, the Daoist hero-god of the Copper Temple (see page 74). His prominent place in a temple of a different religion is explained by his local popularity and the eclectic nature of Buddhism in China. Behind the temple's trinity of Buddhas and a high, finely worked wooden pavilion, stands an altar to Guanyin, facing the rear. Here Yunnan's favourite goddess fulfills her role as Deliverer of Sons,

holding out an unmistakably male baby to newlyweds and barren couples. Beside her stand Zishi, the Daoist, and Wen Sheng, the God of Literature, clad in yellow. These two anticipate the non-Buddhist shrines awaiting on the final stretch of the mountainside.

A 2-kilometre (1.25-mile) walk brings you to the end of the paved road and the climax of Western Hill, **Sanqing Temple** (Sanqingge) and the **Dragon Gate** (Longmen). Half way along, a short distance to the right, lies an old cemetery with many traditional tombs and gravestones. A late addition contains the ashes of Nie Er, the young musician who composed China's present national anthem. He was drowned tragically in Japan in 1936 at the age of 24.

At the end of the road, a long flight of steps ascends to the Pavilion of the Three Pure Ones (Sanqingge), a collection of almost vertical buildings stacked against the face of the mountain. Unfortunately, little is left in their interior except for the central Sanqing pavilion, where three statues of Zishi present him as a black-faced heavenly potentate as well as the familiar warrior god. Sanqing was originally built in the early 14th century as a summer resort for a Mongol prince of the Yuan Dynasty. Renovated 400 years later as a Daoist shrine, it now contains a large teahouse with a splendid view and gives a welcome pause before the final climb.

A stone path leads up past a series of caves and grottoes to the Air Corridor, a tunnel chipped out of living rock. At the far end, it opens out through a stone archway to a temple eyrie on the side of a sheer cliff. The characters *long men* (dragon gate) are inscribed in red and gold upon the arch.

In the year 1781, an impoverished Daoist monk named Wu Laiqing from Sanqing Temple began chipping his way up the cliff with hammer and chisel, motivated by profound devotion. After his death, two pious gentlemen from the region continued his project, aided by villagers from the foot of the mountain. Working day and night in rain or shine, hanging from ropes, they inched the route precariously upward to a natural cliff-top platform, completing Wu Laiqing's visionary plan in 1853. The breathtaking view from the final terrace is one of the great sights of southwest China.

A shrine in the rock wall, called Attainment of Heaven Cave, holds the lively golden image of Kui Xing, the patron God of Scholars. He rides a dragon-fish while heroically brandishing a calligraphy brush — as though to confirm that 'the pen is mightier than the sword' — and blithely balances a potted pomegranate plant, the symbol of long-lasting success, on the sole of his foot. Candidates for the all-important imperial examinations struggled up Western Hill to pray for his help. He is flanked by Wen Cheng, the God of Literature, and Guan Gong, the God of War and Justice. Symbols of bounty, happiness and longevity surround the trio.

Cranes and peaches, representing long life, adorn the ceiling. Phoenixes and peacocks, chess-boards and horses, stand for power and intellectual pleasure. Coloured clouds represent happiness and prosperity. High above the cave, the stone head of a benign old man peers down from a niche. He is none other than Laozi (Lao-Tse), the founder of Daoism.

This particular gathering of gods, sages and emblems symbolized the ambitions of candidates aspiring to high office in the imperial bureaucracy or the army. Successful scholars have left grateful poems and inscriptions along the route above Sanqing. A few failed candidates leapt to their death in despair from the top of Dragon Gate.

An alternative route back to Kunming from the Western Hill follows a steep path straight down the mountain. It starts from the paved road close to Sanqingge and comes out at Dragon Gate Village at the base. From here you can see a long, narrow causeway extending out into Dianchi Lake. Go to its end, where you will find a medieval-style ferry consisting of a wooden boat punted by the cheerful womenfolk of a local peasant family. Upon landing after a five-minute ride, walk east on a clearly marked path by the water's edge to the resort village of Haigen (see below). At the main road you can pick up bus Number 24 for the 10-kilometre (6-mile) ride back to Kunming.

Daguan Park (Daguan Gongyuan)

This large, lake-filled park lies 3 kilometres (1.8 miles) southwest of Kunming at the end of the Number 4 bus line. Built in 1690 by Emperor Kangxi, its rambling, willowed causeways and hump-backed bridges all centre on Daguan Pavilion. Daguan means 'grand view'. True to its name, the three-storey pavilion provides a spectacular view across sparkling Dianchi Lake to the distant Western Hill.

On the pavilion's lakeside facade, two long inscriptions flank a false entranceway, forming a single poem. Written by Sun Ranweng, a famous Qing-Dynasty scholar, this great couplet of 180 characters is one of Yunnan Province's most valued cultural treasures. The first half, on the right, praises the beautiful scenery around Kunming, characterizing local mountains and extolling nature in a sunny, optimistic mood. The second half, on the left, traces 2,000 years of Yunnan's history, commemorating its rulers and warriors, battles and victories. It ends, however, on a melancholy, philosophical note.

Where are they now? . . . neither the setting sun nor the rising fog casts a glance at the crumbling monuments and dilapidated tombstones. What alone remains through eternity are the twinkling lights of the fishermen's boats, the lines of wild geese in the calm autumnal sky, the ringing bell of a distant monastery and the frost that stealthily sets upon the lake's shore.

Bamboo Temple (Qiongzhusi)

On the wooded slopes of Yu'an Hill, 12 kilometres (7.5 miles) northwest of Kunming, stands this author's favourite temple. A direct bus goes daily from the Yunnan Hotel (on Guanghua Jie, diagonally across from the Hongxing Theatre), or you can take bus Number 7 from the Western Station depot as far as Hei Lin Pu, then hike 4 kilometres (2.5 miles) up to your destination. The Bamboo Temple offers the best introduction to Buddhist art and architecture in the region because of its completeness and relative simplicity.

Legend tells that two princes went hunting in the hills outside Kunming in the year 638. A magical rhinoceros led them deep into a forest where it suddenly disappeared. In its stead emerged a group of strange-looking monks carrying staves of bamboo. They too vanished in a purple cloud, but not before leaving their walking sticks planted in the ground. These promptly sprouted leaves and within a day had become an entire grove of special *qiong* bamboo. Here the devout brothers founded a Buddhist temple to honour the miraculous encounter. In fact, the temple, representing the Chan (Zen) sect, has been destroyed and rebuilt many times. The present dimensions seem to date from around 1280, during the reign of Kublai Khan.

The monastery stands on a high stone terrace made from the foundations of earlier temples. A narrow forecourt holds two majestic 450-year-old cypress trees. The entrance hall contains statues of the four guardian kings. On the right of the main courtyard reside the Bamboo Temple's most renowned attractions — 500 finely crafted, idiosyncratic statues of *luohans*. Li Guangxiu, a Sichuanese sculptor of wide renown, appalled the conservatives of his time by introducing this traditional Buddhist folk art into temple architecture between 1884 and 1890, while overseeing the restoration of the temple. The painted clay figures were modelled after real personalities and each life-like caricature embodies a Buddhist virtue. Popular belief claims that, by beginning with any statue and counting down the row to your right as far as the number of your age, you will stop at the *luohan* who best exemplifies your inner self.

The main temple building holds three large Buddha statues — Sakyamuni, the historical Buddha in the middle, the Medicine Buddha on the left, and Amitabha, Lord of the Western Paradise, on the right. Local Buddhists pray and offer incense in front of the three images. Against the left (east) wall of the hall stands a stone stele dating from 1314. It is an imperial decree from the Yuan emperor instructing the temple's abbot to collect Buddhist classics and spread the religion. Written in Mongolian script with a translation into vernacular Chinese, it shows that this must have been a highly influential and politically important temple in the 14th century.

Basic Format of Temples

In spite of variations in size, detail and topography, most temples in Yunnan follow the same layout. An entrance hall leads into an open courtyard bounded on the sides by monastic living quarters and galleries. The main temple stands at the rear with one or two additional temple buildings behind it. In mountainous Yunnan, the complex is often on several levels up a hillside. The temple usually faces south with the entrance at the lowest level, flanked by two guardian figures, either animal or demonic.

The entrance hall usually contains a fat, laughing Buddha and four giant kings, guardians of the four directions. East is white, and he carries a lute. South is blue, and he carries a sword. West is red, and he carries a pagoda or a pearl. North is orange, and he carries a stylized Buddhist banner. The chief of the Four Kings is East.

Courtyards vary greatly, depending on the site, but they commonly hold ancient, sacred trees, a garden and sometimes a pool or fountain.

The main temple normally has central statues of three aspects of the Buddha, or of a single Buddha and two of his disciples. They may be attended by any number of figures representing bodhisattvas, disciples and mythological beings. Behind the main statues there is often a shrine to Guanyin, the Chinese Goddess of Mercy.

The second or third temple building often gives access to a confusing maze of outbuildings, small courtyards, vegetable gardens and so on.

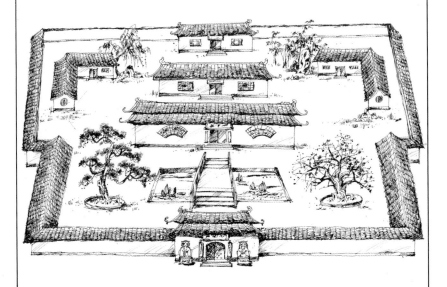

Black Dragon Pool (Heilongtan) and Botanical Garden (Zhiwuyuan)

This park and the ajdacent botanical garden lie in the Wulao Hills, 17 kilometres (10 miles) northwest of Kunming. There is regular service by bus Number 9 from the Chuanxingulou bus depot on Beijing Lu.

The wooded park with its Black Dragon Pool is the site of a restored Ming-Dynasty temple, once the biggest Daoist (Taoist) centre in southwest China. According to legend, the pool originally contained ten violently destructive dragons. Around the year 750 a reclusive scholar named Lu Dongbin mastered the secrets of Daoism and thereupon set out across China to slay dragons and demons. Reaching the pool, he killed nine of the dragons with his sword but allowed the tenth, a small black one, to remain in the pool on condition that it work for the benefit of mankind. Lu Dongbin is honoured as one of the Daoist Eight Immortals, easily recognized in pictures by his sword and fly-whisk. He is the patron saint of Chinese barbers.

The Daoist temple, perched on a hillside overlooking the pool, is built on three levels. The first contains famous, ancient trees in its courtyards — a Tang-Dynasty plum tree, a Song-Dynasty cypress, a Ming-Dynasty camellia and a Qing-Dynasty magnolia. In front of the temple building is a gigantic bronze *ding*, a tripodal incense burner decorated with the eight Daoist trigrams.

The second level building now serves as an art gallery for scroll brush-paintings. The top level is dilapidated but fun to explore.

A seven-minute walk from Black Dragon Pool's entrance leads straight to the Kunming Botanical Garden. The entrance to the garden is through a small gate on the left, directly across the road from the imposing entrance to the Botanical Institute. The meticulously kept gardens contain plant specimens from all over Yunnan Province, but is most widely known for its collection of camellias, Yunnan pine (*Pinus yunnanensis*), rhododendrons and azaleas. Greenhouses are at the far end. It is a very attractive, well-laid-out botanical garden.

Copper Temple or Golden Temple (Jindian)

This unique Daoist temple lies 11 kilometres (7 miles) northeast of Kunming. It can be reached by bus Number 10 from the Chuanxingulou bus depot on Beijing Lu. By car, it is 10 kilometres (6 miles) from Black Dragon Pool, heading southeast on Longtou Jie. Situated in a pine forest atop Phoenix Song Mountain, the temple requires a climb up a very long flight of stone steps, punctuated by three 'Heavenly Gates'. A fourth gate brings visitors to the entrance of the temple grounds.

Gardens and galleries flank a central path leading to a miniature, medieval city wall complete with a typical gate tower, bell tower and drum tower. Inside, on a terrace of finest Dali marble with elegantly carved railings, stands the little copper temple itself. In Chinese it is still known as the Golden Temple because, when first built, the burnished copper gleamed like gold.

In 1604, the governor of Yunnan and some powerful nobles wished to honour the Daoist hero-god Zishi who was supposed to live at the northern extremity of the universe. They built the Copper Temple to represent his city-palace there. Three decades later, the temple was transported intact to Jizushan, a holy mountain in western Yunnan (see page 123). In 1670, a duplicate temple was cast in deliberate defiance of China's new Manchu emperor, to whom the copper was owed as tribute. This second temple was destroyed in the mid-19th century, during Yunnan's great Muslim rebellion. A new temple was built from parts of the duplicate in 1890. The walls, columns, rafters, roof-tiles, altar, altar-hangings, even the banner near the gate tower, are all made of copper. The whole structure weighs more than 300 tons and stands 6.5 metres (21 feet) high.

Outlying buildings, containing art galleries and a teahouse, are not of great interest, except to the thirsty. At the summit of the mountain behind the temple, a bizarre, ugly tower, built in 1984, holds a giant bronze bell, so massive that its rim is a full hand span in thickness. Its decorations identify it as a Buddhist relic, not originally a part of this Daoist temple. The huge camellia tree near the temple is 600 years old; in the month of February it produces hundreds of magnificent red blossoms — a sight that should not be missed by springtime visitors to Kunming.

Yunnan Observatory (Yunnan Tianwentai)

An important centre for astronomy is located on Phoenix Hill, 10 kilometres (6 miles) east of Kunming. It is best reached by car under the auspices of CITS. Over 2,000 metres (6,550 feet) above sea level, the sprawling complex of buildings and silver domes commands an impressive view across the plain and Dianchi Lake to the far distant Western Hill by day, while its telescopes give a clear view of the skies by night.

The Observatory, administered by the Chinese Academy of Sciences, has sections for radio astronomy, solar physics, stellar physics, celestial mechanics and astrometry. A technical laboratory works with new instruments and computers. The one-metre optical telescope — the second largest in China next to Shanghai's — is in use approximately 200 nights out of the year. A satellite tracking station and a parabolic radio telescope complete the installation.

The Yunnan Observatory conducts guided tours for the public with lectures, a visit to the small exhibition hall and night-time observation of the moon, planets and stars through a 35-centimetre telescope. Arrangements can be made through CITS.

Sights around Lake Dianchi

Lake Dianchi, 340 square kilometres (132 square miles), is the largest lake in Yunnan and the sixth largest in China. Its length is 40 kilometres (25 miles) and the width at its widest point is 14 kilometres (9 miles).

The lake, capable of tossing up violent storms, is especially beautiful when winds subside and it reflects the ethereal light of dawn or sunset. The Chinese describe the lake's moods as 'virility seasoned with tenderness'. Its shores are dotted with small fishing hamlets surrounded by fertile fields. High rectangular sails ribbed with bamboo battens propel ancient-style wooden boats across the water. Fishing boats carry a single sail; big three-masted hulls transport rock from lakeside quarries — just as they have done for 2,000 years. In any weather, the mountain-girded lake is a splendid sight and a day trip around its shores is well worth the effort.

Interesting places to stop as you follow a clockwise route around Dianchi are listed below. All can be reached by bus. However, for convenience and flexibility while sightseeing we recommend hiring a car for the day.

Haigeng

This lakeside resort lies 10 kilometres (6 miles) directly south of Kunming. Bus Number 24 departs regularly from East Station and terminates at Haigeng. It is also an easy bicycle ride. Along the small, picturesque road between Kunming and the lake you will pass through typical farming villages and pleasant countryside.

Haigeng is known as 'Kunming's Riviera' and with an enormous stretch of the imagination you might think it vaguely approaches that. In the past few years the area has been spruced up and is extremely popular with local young people during the weekends. There is a roller-skating rink, a small man-made lake with boats for hire, and numerous small shops and vendors selling everything from boiled eggs and sunflower seeds to tinned fruit and beer. The main attraction is a long, willow-lined esplanade along the lake front. Two long cement jetties run out into the lake. The water is not particularly clean but on a hot day it attracts many swimmers. On week days, when there are no crowds, Haigeng is a nice place for a picnic. For the energetic, it is possible to walk from Haigeng to the top of Western Hill, or vice versa.

Haigeng has gained some publicity in China due to an Olympic village nearby where the nation's top athletes receive training in the high, pure air of Yunnan.

Xiaobanqiao

This country market town lies 12 kilometres (7.5 miles) southeast of Kunming. On bus Number 12, it is the fifth stop from East Station to Chenggong. Sunday is market day, when costumed peasants, villagers, craftsmen and fishermen from the neighbouring countryside gather for an open-air market, setting up stalls elbow to elbow down the streets and alleys. It is interesting and fun to take part in a genuine, rustic event and you may find something amazing or unique to buy: a pair of flowered peasant shoes, a jade-inlaid pipe, some lovingly crafted hand-tools, a baby pig or an apron embroidered with cranes and camellias.

The Eastern Shore

After Xiaobanqiao the road leads south for 14 kilometres (9 miles) to the big town of Chenggong, where the main road to the Stone Forest branches off to the left. (Do not take it on this trip.) Markets take place in this town, too, but they tend to be more modern and less colourful. The area south of Chenggong is known for its apple, peach and pear orchards. The succulent pearl pear (*baozhuli*) is a local speciality, much prized for its flavour.

Along the whole stretch of the road heading south, small roads lead enticingly off to the right towards the lake. To follow any one of them is to enter the untouched world of rural Yunnan. You may find a little teahouse, fishermen mending nets, an ancient, forgotten pagoda or a tiny harbour with a boat landing its catch.

The old county town of Jincheng, 14 kilometres (9 miles) beyond Chenggong, is a good place to stop for a cup of tea. Five kilometres west of it is the archaeological site of Shizhaishan, a hill where 48 Bronze-Age tombs yielded a trove of art treasures in 1955.

Passing around the southern end of the lake, the next sizeable town is Jinning, formally called Kunyang, birthplace of the great 15th-century explorer Zheng He (see page 81). The white skull-caps of the Muslims, the black turbans of the Han, the fur-fringed hats of the Yi, all reflect the ethnic mixture in this area. Zheng He, the eunuch admiral, was himself a Muslim. He is the town's most revered native son. Each year, his descendants gather here from all parts of China to celebrate the Muslim festival of Qurban Bayran.

A museum honouring Zheng He, his family and his accomplishments stands north of Jinning at Moon Hill (Yueshan), which is also known as Zheng He Park. It is a well-kept, impressive museum for such a small town and worth a stop. Bus Number 21 from Jinning has its terminus near the park, 6 kilometres (4 miles) north of the town.

The Eunuch Admiral

In the year 1381, a ten-year-old Muslim boy named Ma Ho played among the fishing boats of his village, Kunyang, and dreamt that Dianchi Lake was a boundless ocean. His father and grandfather had made the pilgrimage to Mecca, at Asia's farthest limit, and had told rousing tales of the seas beyond China. The distinguished family, descended from an early Mongol governor of Yunnan, still remained loyal to the dynasty of Kublai Khan, and helped Yunnan put up resistance to the new Ming Dynasty that had seized power in China.

That year, a Ming army stormed into Yunnanfu, as Kunming was then called, and encircled Dianchi Lake, sweeping up captives. Ma Ho was seized, along with other boys, castrated, and sent into the army as an orderly. By the age of 20, the bright lad had become a junior officer, skilled at war and diplomacy. His abilities won him influential friends who helped him move to Nanjing, China's capital, during a turbulent period of wars and revolts. There he gained power and prestige as a court eunuch and the emperor gave him a new name — Cheng Ho or, as now spelled, Zheng He.

For 300 years, China had been extending its seaborne power, building up widespread commerce, importing spices, aromatics and raw materials from different parts of Asia. The arts of shipbuilding and navigation reached their height during the early Ming Dynasty. In 1405, the emperor appointed Zheng He as 'Commander-in-Chief of All Missions to the Western Seas', whereupon the eunuch admiral set sail on a mission of exploration and trade. He took 62 ships carrying 27,800 men — the biggest naval fleet in the whole world at that time. It was the first of the seven far-flung voyages that took him to the Indian Ocean, Persia, Arabia and the east coast of Africa.

On his fourth trip, Zheng He visited every major port of South and Southeast Asia and brought back envoys from more than 30 states to forge diplomatic relations and pay homage to the emperor of China. After the ambassadors had resided for six years in the new capital of Beijing, Zheng He made another voyage and took them all home again.

Thanks to Zheng He's genius, China held power over much of maritime Asia for half a century. However, China never established a trading empire, in contrast to the European nations who soon began exploring the earth's oceans, too. Instead, Zheng He's discoveries encouraged Chinese emigrants to settle in foreign countries, where their communities have flourished ever since.

Zheng He's atlases, logs and charts bequeathed a priceless record to the world and made maritime history. On his seventh and last voyage, between 1431 and 1433, Zheng He revisited all the distant places he had discovered 25 years earlier. He died in 1435, honoured throughout China but best beloved by the people of the southwest in the land of his birth, Yunnan.

Zheng He Park and Museum (Zheng He Gongyuan)

The focus of this sprawling, somewhat run-down park is the museum itself, housed in an elaborately reconstructed Buddhist temple. The only sight worth mentioning in the park is the tomb of Zheng He's father, the *hajji*, which lies near the walkway. The original 600-year-old stele tells the family's history and exploits in Chinese characters that are still legible.

The first room of the museum contains rubbings from many different steles telling of Zheng He's deeds. The most important is from the 1,170-character stele, the Zheng He Inscription Stone, which stands in the coastal city of Quanzhou in Fujian Province, chronicling his seven great voyages. The second room holds examples of the Chinese products which Zheng He took in his ships to trade abroad, notably Ming pottery known as Dragon Spring, or *longquan*, ware. Examples have been found in Java, Sri Lanka, Africa and many other points along his routes. This room also displays photographs of these and other sites where his ships touched shore, as well as some indifferent modern paintings recreating scenes from Zheng He's diplomatic encounters.

Upstairs there are fine, clear diagrams and charts of Zheng He's huge ships, some capable of carrying over 500 men. The dimensions of their towering masts are shown, along with the anchors and sails. Navigational instruments include a complicated compass. The walls are covered with good maps that show in detail the extent of his trips and landfalls.

Haikou and Baiyukou

Heading north along the western shore of Dianchi Lake, the first big town is Haikou, several kilometres inland. It is an unprepossessing, industrial town redeemed by the numerous restaurants along the main road which offer good, simple fare. At Haikou, the Praying Mantis River (Tanglang Jiang) carries the waters of Dianchi Lake towards the Yangzi River at the border of Sichuan Province, then on to the East China Sea.

Baiyukou, a resort centred on a big sanatorium, lies on the lake 10 kilometres (6 miles) north of Haikou. The spacious health centre, set aside for Kunming's workers, has attractive gardens and grounds running down to the water's edge; these are open to the public. A handsome stone mansion, the country retreat of a pre-revolutionary mayor of Kunming, has been appropriated by the sanitorium. Causeways lined by willow trees, symbols of spring and friendship, enclose miniature lakes. There are pleasant walks among pine and eucalyptus woods behind Baiyukou, and caves to explore.

Bus Number 33 from Nantaiqiao Station in Kunming terminates at Baiyukou. There is also a ferry boat that makes a round trip from Kunming to Baiyukou once a day. If you are not in a hurry, the water route is a picturesque and leisurely way to make the trip, either coming or going.

Energetic games are a favourite part of minority festivals. A 'see-saw' of the Hani people forms the centre-piece of a wild game that includes clowns, slapstick, and dizzying feats of strength.

Guanyinshan Temple (Guanyinshansi)

From Baiyukou, looking north along the shore, you can see a ruined pagoda on a promontory named Guanyin Shan. On the hillside behind the pagoda stands a charming little Ming-Dynasty temple, hidden in the woods. A steep, unpaved track runs up to it from the left side of the main road. Two monks and three nuns take care of the Buddhist shrine, which is dedicated to Guanyin, the Goddess of Mercy. They welcome visitors to the main temple building, the most ancient in the small complex. Its worn stone floor, banners of orange, red, pink and yellow silk, the burning candles and incense all imbue the small temple with warmth and intimacy. Peasants are likely to drop in, to place offerings of tangerines and wine before the Buddha statues and especially before the goddess herself.

A brief walk down to the ruined pagoda, Guanyin Ta, gives a magnificent view of red mountains, blue water and innumerable shades of green in the fields below. The highly visible pagoda was built centuries ago at this spot to be seen from all directions as a beacon to the Buddhist faithful. It was ruined, like many Buddhist monuments, during the Muslim rebellion in the mid-19th century.

To end the trip, you can take bus Number 33 north along the main road. The distance is 18 kilometres (11 miles) from Guanyin Shan to the bus stop at the base of Western Hill, and 26 kilometres (16 miles) back to Kunming.

If you are planning to make the circular trip around Lake Dianchi by public bus, it would be advisable to study the map on page 66 first. At least five different buses ply the regular routes, all terminating at different towns around the lake. Bus Number 12 from East Station terminates at Chenggong, with a stop at Xiaobanqiao. Bus Number 13 from Nantaiqiao Station terminates at Jincheng with a stop at Chenggong. Bus Number 14 from Nantaiqiao Station ends at Jinning, but bypasses Xiaobanqiao. Irregular local buses go between Jinning and Haikou where bus Number 15 takes an inland route around the back of Western Hill back to Kunming. Bus Number 33 runs between Baiyukou and Kunming on the lakeside road.

Anning Hot Springs (Anning Wenquan)

The bustling county seat of Anning lies 34 kilometres (21 miles) southwest of Kunming on the famous old Burma Road that now serves as the main east-west highway of Yunnan. The hot springs are at the centre of a spa 8 kilometres (5 miles) north of Anning. Bus Number 18 goes from Nantaiqiao Station in Kunming directly to the hot springs.

The springs were discovered two thousand years ago in the Han Dynasty and Anning has been a favourite bathing spot ever since. Foreigners may find it a far cry from Baden Baden, but the happy grins of parboiled Chinese will attest to its continuing popularity. The clear, odour-less mineral water bubbles up at an average of 42°C (102°F). Several guest houses rent out tiled bathing rooms at Rmb5 for single occupancy or Rmb3 for a shared room, with towels and slippers included.

A trip to Anning should certainly include visits to two nearby Buddhist sites: **Caoxi Temple** and the **Fahua Temple Grottoes**.

Caoxi Temple is 2 kilometres south of the hot springs. It is the only remaining Song-Dynasty (960−1279) structure in the Kunming area. Legend says that a monk in AD 502 was so beguiled by the quality of the water that he founded a temple there. The temple's subsequent history included patronage by Huineng, one of Chan (Zen) Buddhism's greatest patriarchs. Among the precious, wooden, Song-Dynasty sculptures, the central Buddha is noted for a remarkable event that takes place once every 60 years. The September full moon that marks China's Mid-Autumn Festival then shines through a small hole in the temple roof, placing a medallion of silvery moonlight on the Buddha's forehead.

The Fahua Temple Grottoes are all that remain of an ancient Song-Dynasty Buddhist temple in the cliffs behind Little Peach Flower Village (Xiao Taohuacun), 5 kilometres (3 miles) east of the town of Anning. Eighteen *luohans* are carved in three vertical rows of different sizes on the east side of the cliff, and near by these holy men are scenes from the Jattaka, folklore tales of the Buddha. To the south of the cliff lies a large reclining Buddha, 4.2 metres (14 feet) long.

Though few tourists take the baths, it is worthwhile to ride down the Burma Road and visit the ancient Buddhist sites around Anning.

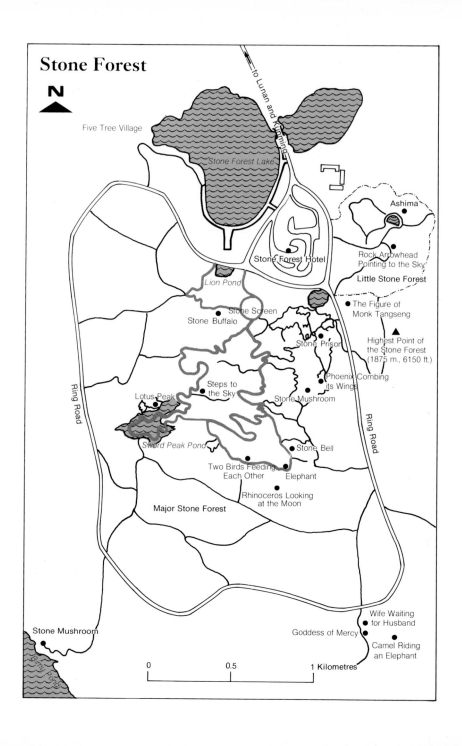

The Stone Forest (Shilin)

The Stone Forest is the name given to an extremely rare geological pheno-menon 126 kilometres (79 miles) southeast of Kunming. It is not a petri-fied forest but 80 hectares (200 acres) of karst limestone pillars in fantastic shapes that, from a distance, resemble a forest. About 270 million years ago, during the Permian Period, this area was covered by water. Later, due to shifts in the earth's crust, the ocean slowly receded while the limestone sea bed rose up to form a tableland. Rain and seeping water ate away at the limestone surface. The stone eroded in different places, causing fissures to open around small pinnacles. In time, acidic rain devoured most of the limestone, leaving the huge, isolated, but densely packed stone pillars that can be seen today in the middle of Lunan County. The Stone Forest, one of the main attractions of Yunnan, is the home of the Sani people, who make up a branch of the Yi tribe.

Getting to the Stone Forest

There are several ways to reach the Stone Forest. Tourist groups travel there by private bus, but there are also numerous public buses bound for the Stone Forest every day. The most convenient public bus leaves from the alley directly west of the Kunming Hotel. The round trip costs Rmb10. Tickets can be bought at the travel desk of the Kunming Hotel. Other, cheaper, buses leave from the Number One Department Store and make a stop on Dongfeng Dong Lu across the street from the Kunming Hotel. A private car, though more expensive, can get to the Stone Forest in less than two hours.

The least known but most interesting way to get to the Stone Forest is to use a combination of train and bus. Early this century, the French built a narrow-guage railway to link their colonial capital of Hanoi, in Indochina, with Kunming. It snakes across craggy mountains and lush valleys on its way southeast to the Vietnamese border, where it now terminates. Tourists can take this charming little train to the county seat of **Yiliang**, two-thirds of the way to the Stone Forest, and travel the remaining 36 kilometres (22.5 miles) by bus. Yiliang's bus station is on the left side of the main road just before the chief intersection as you walk into town.

Train Number 501 leaves from Kunming's North Station (see map on page 34) at 8.35 am and chugs along at barely 40 kilometres (25 miles) per hour, allowing you to see some of Yunnnan's most pleasant countryside. Small stations are built in French style, with painted shutters and steep roofs. After crossing a high, barren mountain pass, the train makes a big curve to the left. Far below, on the right, is **Yangzong Hai**, a wild, blue lake about 15 kilometres (9 miles) from Yiliang. A strong walker might

want to alight at Yangzong Hai Station, walk down the sparsely inhabited mountain to the lake shore, have a picnic, then walk on to Yiliang.

It is a medium-sized town at the centre of a rich agricultural area, small enough to explore in a couple of hours. The market along its main street is a full-blown country event. The citadel at the centre of the old town gives a fine view over curly-eaved roofs, temples and lanes.

To return from the Stone Forest, several bus companies operate routes to Kunming. Buses leave from the Stone Forest bus station (see map on page 90) between 2 and 4 in the afternoon.

Hotels in the Stone Forest

Stone Forest Hotel
(Shilin Binguan)
Lunan County

石林宾馆
路南县

Double room Rmb50, dormitory Rmb10

Situated within sight of the eerie limestone pillars, this pleasant, rambling, somewhat rustic hotel has 76 double rooms with private bathrooms attached. These can be booked through CITS in Kunming. There are a number of cheaper rooms with up to six beds in each, but these have no toilet. The main restaurant seats over 300 people and is geared to serve large groups. Individuals can get meals here as well, though there is sometimes a delay. Western and Chinese breakfasts are available.

The Stone Forest Hotel is frequently full between the months of August and October. At this time, when no beds are available, many visitors are forced to make a one-day trip and return to Kunming in the afternoon. This is a pity because the Stone Forest is at its most beautiful in the soft light of sunset and sunrise. A bed can always be found in the hostels surrounding the bus station near the turn-off from the highway. These hostels are spartan and very cheap.

The main hotel has a resthouse (*xiuxishi*) which contains a bar and performance hall for the nightly song and dance show of the local Sani minority. This is well worth attending. Numerous shops in and around the hotel sell Sani handicrafts, especially embroidered clothing, bags, shoes, and children's hats.

Sights at the Stone Forest

As could be expected with such a special area, legends abound in Sani folklore. Its creation legend is a Promethean fable. A Sani youth named Jinfeng Roga was ambitious and bold, but also caring. He wanted to save the local farmers from drought by building a great dam to catch the waters. One night he sneaked into the crypt of the gods and stole their talisman, a magic whip capable of moving mountains. All through the night, the hero drove rocky hills like a flock of sheep towards the town of Yiliang, his chosen dam site. But the crowing cocks signalled daybreak before his task was finished, and the talisman lost its power. The hills stopped fast and became the Stone Forest. Jinfeng Roga was soon captured and brutally murdered by the gods. His martyrdom is recalled by long cracks in the rocks, said to be the whip weals inflicted on his body.

Another, more romantic legend, is told throughout Yunnan in song, story and dance-drama. It concerns a beautiful Sani girl named Ashima and her brother Ahei. Ashima and her family lived happily among their tribe until a wicked magician carried her off to his castle. After many trials and tribulations, Ahei rescued his sister. With freedom almost in their grasp, the siblings fled through the 12 mighty crags of the Stone Forest. Here a flood, unleashed by the magician, swept Ashima away, separating her forever from her brother and the idyllic life of her people. Ashima's aura appeared above the Stone Forest and her spirit lived on there as an echo. Ashima has been immortalized in the natural formation of a limestone rock, one which resembles a young girl, within the Little Stone Forest.

The Chinese delight in projecting their imagination onto nature. Almost every prominent peak in the rock jungle bears a name, such as Mother and Son Going for a Walk, Rhinoceros Looking at the Moon, Phoenix Preening its Wings, or A Camel Riding an Elephant. The map on page 90 shows the location of the hotel, the other buildings and the major walking routes through the Main Stone Forest and the Little Stone Forest.

A gravel road about 7 kilometres (4.5 miles) long encircles the whole area. It can take you away from crowded tourist areas into open countryside with the Stone Forest forming a backdrop. On the northern stretch there is a sizeable lake and, nearby, Five Tree Village, a typical Sani settlement well known for its amiable craftsmen and musicians. Outside the southern limit of the circular road there are several clusters of natural stone sculptures. Paths lead southward towards rarely visited traditional Sani villages. If you leave the gravel road, you might consider taking a stick to ward off unfriendly dogs.

The colourful Sani people around the Stone Forest are highly attuned

to tourists but this has not brought about a significant debasement of their culture. Their handicrafts, especially bags and clothing with beautiful embroidery and appliqué work, are on sale in profusion around the hotel. Performances of rousing Sani dances, music and songs are held each evening in the hotel's theatre. These are surprisingly good and everyone likes to share in the fun.

The highlight of each year at the Stone Forest is the Torch Festival, which takes place on 24 June of the lunar calendar (about late July or early August by our Gregorian calendar). It is a gala of horse-racing, bullfighting, wrestling, music, drinking and dancing, drawing together Sani people from all over Lunan County. The climax at nightfall is a torchlight parade through the Stone Forest accompanied by elephant drums, flutes and Sani lutes.

The town of **Lunan** lies 6 kilometres (3.75 miles) southwest of the Stone Forest. It can be reached by heading back along the Kunming road for 4 kilometres (2.5 miles), then taking the only paved road to the left. The market buzzes with activity, and this is the departure point for a 25-kilometre (15-mile) trip to **Dadishui**, Yunnan's largest waterfall.

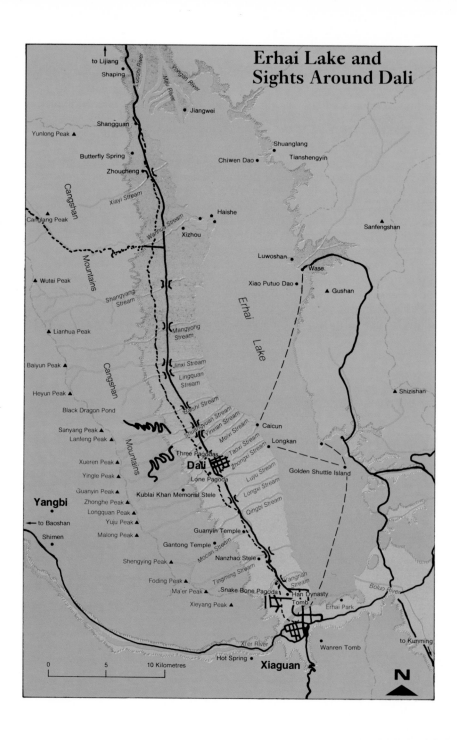

Erhai Lake and
Sights Around Dali

to Lijiang

Shaping

Jiangwei

Shangguan

Yunlong Peak ▲

Butterfly Spring

Shuanglang

Tianshengyin

Chiwen Dao ●

Zhoucheng

Cangshan

Xiayi Stream

Haishe

Canglang Peak ▲

Wanhua Stream

Xizhou

Sanfengshan ▲

Luwoshan ●

Wase

Wutai Peak ▲

Xiao Putuo Dao ●

Gushan ▲

Shangyang Stream

Mountains

Lianhua Peak ▲

Mangyohg Stream

Erhai

Baiyun Peak ▲

Jinxi Stream

Lingquan Stream

Lake

Heyun Peak ▲

Bashi Stream

Shizishan ▲

Black Dragon Pond

Shuangyuan Stream

Yinxian Stream

Caicun ●

Sanyang Peak ▲

Meixi Stream

Longkan

Lanfeng Peak ▲

Three Pagodas

Taoxi Stream

Xueren Peak ▲

Dali

Zhongxi Stream

Golden Shuttle Island

Yingle Peak ▲

Lone Pagoda

Luju Stream

Guanyin Peak ▲

Kublai Khan Memorial Stele

Longxi Stream

Yangbi

Zhonghe Peak ▲

Qingbi Stream

Longquan Peak ▲

→ to Baoshan

Yuju Peak ▲

Guanyin Temple ●

Shimen

Malong Peak ▲

Gantong Temple ●

Mocan Stream

Shengying Peak ▲

Nanzhao Stele ●

Foding Peak ▲

Tingming Stream

Yangnan Stream

Ma'er Peak ▲

Snake Bone Pagoda ●

Han Dynasty Tomb

Boluo River

Xieyang Peak ▲

Erhai Park

Xi'er River

to Kunming

0   5   10 Kilometres

Wanren Tomb ●

Hot Spring ●

Xiaguan

N

Dali

Dali, the capital of the Dali Bai Autonomous Prefecture west of Kunming, is the historic home of the Bai minority, one of Yunnan's most numerous and prosperous ethnic groups. The name Dali refers to both the old stone town and the surrounding region. The old town of weathered gray granite stands at 1,900 metres (6,232 feet) on a long, narrow rice plain between the Azure Mountains (Cangshan) and the unpolluted Ear Lake (Erhai), a natural configuration that seems specially designed for a good, bountiful life. In late winter, when fields of brilliant yellow rape-seed glow between snow-capped mountains and the sapphire blue lake, one can agree with the Bai that theirs is the most blessed spot on earth.

The lake, named for its ear-like shape, lies in a geological fault between parallel mountain ranges, south of the great river trenches of the eastern Himalayas. Erhai Lake, 41 kilometres (30 miles) long and 3 to 9 kilometres (2 to 5 miles) wide, is part of the Mekong River system. The small Xi'er River, fed by glaciers and snow water, enters the lake at its northern end through Dragon's Head Pass. It leaves the lake's southwest corner serenely by a canal at the big town of Xiaguan, but soon tumbles boisterously through the Cangshan at Dragon's Tail Pass, a cleft so narrow that a boulder stuck between cliffs forms a natural bridge above it.

The Cangshan range stands like a wall behind Dali's plain, with a long, looping skyline shaped by 19 peaks averaging about 4,000 metres (13,000 feet). Unlike the craggy ranges piled up elsewhere in western Yunnan, the Cangshan alone is made of granite, thrusting up through the earth's limestone crust. Its rich deposits of high quality marble add to Dali's prosperity, and it provides the deep, black earth of the plain at its foot, a contrast to Yunnan's typical red clay.

The plain, 56 kilometres (35 miles) long but only 3 or 4 kilometres (2 or 3 miles) wide, is watered by 18 perennial mountain streams, which farmers channel to every plot and terrace. The 19 peaks and 18 streams are the emblems of Dali. Towns and villages perch on the mountain's lower slopes or on the lakeshore, keeping the entire plain for agriculture. Rice grows abundantly in summer and autumn; beans and wheat are secondary crops. In former times, Dali thrived on its winter opium crops, until the Chinese government suppressed the trade in the 1930s.

The eastern shore of Erhai Lake is totally different. The low, barren, Red Rocky Mountains (Hongshishan) rise directly from the water, with small villages clinging to the foothills. Although receiving little rain, the sparse, red soil is good for peach and pear orchards, wherever it exists. Fishing is the main occupation of this shore, for Erhai Lake contains more than 40 varieties of fish. Bai boat owners also transport building materials around the lake, and nowadays match the Bai farmers in prosperity.

Bai means 'white' but the origin of this name is not clear. It has nothing to do with skin colour or colour of dress — Bai women wear a variety of brightly coloured costumes. They call themselves Speakers of the White Language, a tongue distinct from Mandarin, or People of the White King, though the king's identity is lost in conflicting myths.

Dali, their ancestral home, is a town of some 12,000 inhabitants. It lies three kilometres (two miles) from the lakeshore, under the highest peak of the Cangshan, roughly in the middle of the plain. The bigger town of Xiaguan, 15 kilometres (9 miles) south, occupies the southwest corner of the lake. Xiaguan began as a trade centre at the crossing of two major caravan routes, linking China with Burma, and eastern Tibet with the tea plantations of southern Yunnan. Xiaguan still remains a more important commercial centre, whereas Dali has historically been a seat of political power.

Dali was the capital of an independent kingdom named Nanzhao during the eighth and ninth centuries, while the Tang Dynasty reigned in China. At its height, Nanzhao conquered much of Burma, attacked parts of Laos and Thailand, and repeatedly invaded China's Sichuan region in a border war that helped to weaken the Tang Dynasty. The royal family of Nanzhao came to an end in 902, when the Chief Minister murdered the infant heir to the throne and proceeded to wipe out all other members of the family as well, initiating decades of turmoil. In 937, a Bai official usurped the throne and renamed the realm the Kingdom of Dali. It prospered for three more centuries, until Kublai Khan conquered it in 1253 and made it an outpost of China.

Under the Song Dynasty (960–1279), China's army faced a grave crisis when it lost its steady supply of horses. Wars in the north deprived it of vast pasturelands and traditional horse-breeding grounds. The Kingdom of Dali provided the solution. Yunnan's breed of strong horses had been known for centuries to the Chinese, who prized the animals for their endurance. About the year 1130, Dali began delivering 1,500 horses a year to the Song government, in exchange for silk, silver and salt.

Fine horses are still traded in Dali. For over a thousand years, the Bai have staged a great annual fair on the open land outside Dali's west gate. The Third Month Fair (Sanyue Jie) takes place in April or early May by the Gregorian calendar. This fair evolved from religious gatherings in which Buddhist monks, disciples and laymen met on the Dali Plain at the time of the third full moon to pray, fast, chant and preach. Fruits and flowers, incense and oil were the main devotional offerings and in time, with the growth of the annual worship festival and subsequent social interchange, trade naturally followed to fulfill the material needs of the faithful. Today, mountain tribes and buyers from many parts of China gather for five days of trading, horse-racing and traditional games. A city of tents and booths springs up, livestock of every sort can be found mooing, bleating and squealing in the animal market, but the fair's greatest drawing power nowadays comes from the rare herbs and medicines that Tibetans and others bring down from the remote mountains on Yunnan's borders. Ranking second to medicines are horses, ridden bareback or in full regalia around a small racetrack to show off their speed and prowess.

With all Dali's prosperity, its famous marble and rich agriculture, with its colour and vigorous life, it is small wonder that the Bai people consider it the best spot in China and never want to leave it.

Getting to Dali

The largest city in the Dali region is **Xiaguan** at the southwest end of Erhai Lake, 15 kilometres (9 miles) south of Dali. All transport goes to Xiaguan first.

The Dali-Erhai Lake region lies exactly 400 kilometres (250 miles) west of Kunming. There are no flights and no trains so the only way to go is by road. This route is the famous Burma Road, which acted as Free China's lifeline to the outside world during World War II. Today it remains the main east-west highway in Yunnan. The trip takes seven or eight hours by car, and a few hours longer by bus. Though this may seem long and rigorous, it is an exciting experience to roll through hills and mountains, occasionally coming out onto broad plains, sharing the road with trucks, jeeps, wheelbarrows, oxen, and donkey carts. The bus stops two or three times en route at food stalls offering seeds, nuts, boiled eggs and noodles in broth. The one main stop during the day is in **Chuxiong**, the centre and administrative capital of Yunnan's Yi minority.

Chuxiong is four hours from Kunming, 185 kilometres (116 miles) along the route. At the numerous restaurants and noodle stalls near the bus stop, passengers rush for a quick, filling lunch before piling back into the bus for the remaining trip. There is not much time for exploring and you will be extremely unpopular with passengers and the irate bus driver if you show up late. However, even a quick look into nearby alleys will give you the flavour of the Yi people and their street markets.

Chuxiong is an 'open' town, so you can stay the night in the government guesthouse. Some sites out of town make this worthwhile for visitors with special interests. Local trips can be arranged with CITS. Besides Yi villages in the countryside where you might be lucky enough to strike a market day or a festival, there are two famous paleontological sites in the region. Dinosaur fossils have been found at **Lufeng**, 80 kilometres (50 miles) back towards Kunming; and Yuanmou Man, China's oldest humanoid ancestor (predating Peking Man by many thousand years) was discovered in this district in 1965. The town of **Yuanmou** lies on the

Kunming-Chengdu railway line 85 kilometres (53 miles) northwest of Chuxiong.

The bus route from Chuxiong to Dali is almost continuously mountainous, except in the broad Changyun Plain. Here, on one of Yunnan's rare flat, fertile areas, Bronze-Age farmers thrived. Changyun has an airstrip that played an important role in the fight against the Japanese during World War II and it may soon be brought into service again for tourists travelling to Dali. A mountain bulwark rises from the plain, the last great obstacle before entering the Dali Bai Autonomous Region. The bus creeps zigzag fashion up precipitous Red Rocky Mountains, offering a superb view. The road finally levels off before reaching the city of Xiaguan.

Buses leave Kunming for Xiaguan several times every morning, the earliest ones departing at 6 am. Tickets can be bought at the CITS travel desk in the lobby of the Kunming Hotel or directly from the Passenger Transport Bus Station (Qiche Keyun Zhan) near the train station at the southern end of Beijing Lu. Large buses are preferable to mini-buses; they are more comfortable and the drivers (generally) more sane. Taxis can also be hired for the fast eight-hour trip but be prepared to pay up to Rmb1.5 per kilometre.

Xiaguan, Yunnan's second largest city, has a population of about half a million. It spreads around the southwestern tip of Erhai Lake and rises part way up the surrounding hills. In contrast to small, charming Dali, 15 kilometres (9 miles) to the north, Xiaguan has a good deal of ugly industrial sprawl and little outstanding architecture. It is the main commercial and transportation centre of western Yunnan and all buses make a stop here.

Most tour groups stay in Xiaguan and make day trips to Dali and the surrounding country.

Hotels in the Dali Region

Xiaguan

Erhai Guesthouse
(Erhai Binguan)

洱海宾馆

This is a deluxe hotel by the standards of this part of the world. It is adequate; there is hot water in the bathrooms and the staff are friendly if not terribly efficient.

Xiaguan Hotel
(Xiaguan Fandian)

下关饭店

Located close to the main bus station on Jianshe Lu, this travellers' hotel is recommended only for those who need to watch their budget.

There is also a hostelry across the road from the bus station's main gate.

Dali

**Number Two
Guesthouse**
(Di Er Zhaodaisuo)
Huguo Lu

第二招待所
护国路

The Number Two Guesthouse is the place to
stay in the town of Dali. Its clientele is young
and broadly international. The popularity of Dali
has forced the guesthouse to expand. It is now an
extensive complex with varying accommodations,
though most guests still prefer to sleep
dormitory-style with three or four beds in each
room. Double rooms are available with private
bathrooms but the quality of plumbing cannot be
guaranteed. The advantages of staying here
rather than in Xiaguan are the camaraderie and
special feeling of living within the old stone
town.

Food and Drink in the Dali Region

Xiaguan

Because of Xiaguan's large Muslim community, many of the restaurants
are halal, offering a good, simple fare of noodles, flat bread, mutton,
beancurd and fried vegetables. A number of restaurants can be found in
the northern part of the city and along Cangshan Xi Lu. Two local
specialities are *erkuai*, a noodle-like dish made from pressed rice, usually
fried with green onions, and dog, euphemistically known in this part of
Yunnan as *diyang*, or 'earth goat'.

Dali

The eating scene in Dali has changed drastically over the past three years
as local entrepreneurs have catered to the tastes of foreigners. Small
restaurants have sprung up and the larger ones have menus in English.
Some favourite places are listed below.

***Restaurants and
teahouses***

Apricot Flower Restaurant (Xinghua
Fandian) Yu'er Lu
杏花饭店

Muslim Restaurant (Huimin Fandian) Huguo
Lu
回民饭店 护国路

Garden Teahouse (Huayuan Chaguan)
Guangwu Lu
花园茶馆

Sights in the Dali Region

Hot Spring (Wenquan)

This hot spring is the focus of a small spa in the tight valley of the Xi'er River, 7 kilometres (4 miles) southwest of Xiaguan. The water is fine and hot. A long, languid soak in the large marble pools, one even called the Emperor's Bath, makes the excursion worthwhile. The facilities are not fancy, but the bathing rooms are clean and private. Take your own slippers and towel.

Tea Factory (Chachang)

The main task of the Yunnan Fragrant Flower Tea Factory is to supply tea to Tibet and the other distant border regions of China. Yunnan tea is especially prized and 80 per cent of this factory's annual production of 1,600 tons ends up in Tibet where the people drink prodigious amounts for hydration, energy, digestion and hospitality.

For ease in transport and barter and to prevent spoilage the tea is steam-pressed into quarter-kilo bricks. This pressed tea (*jin cha*) was formerly made into enormous two-kilo and four-kilo bricks; these can now only be seen in the factory's museum. Other exhibits include a dozen major types of tea products and marvellous 'special issue' bricks embossed in Chinese, English and Russian, which were produced up until 20 years ago.

In recent times, the factory has begun exporting tea to Europe. Small, bell-shaped bricks of highest quality tea, called *tuocha*, have gained great popularity because of its apparent efficacy as a weight reducer. Arrangements to visit the tea factory in Xiaguan must be made through CITS.

Erhai Park (Erhai Gongyuan)

Xiaguan's most attractive park stretches along Tuanshan Hill at the southern end of Erhai Lake. Royal deer belonging to the Nanzhao kings used to graze here 1,200 years ago, and on a clear day it is easy to see why the spot was chosen for a modern park. The view looks directly up the lake for miles. To the west, fading away majestically, all 19 peaks of the Cangshan range are visible.

The park is well-kept, dotted with pavilions, staircases and flower gardens, and it has a teahouse. A small but meticulously maintained botanical garden lies at the eastern base of the hill, reached by a long descending flight of stairs. Its outstanding collection of camellias, magnolias and azaleas gives an idea of the botanical riches that are native to the Cangshan Mountains. Sometimes fishing fleets of 20 or 30 boats are pulled up at the base of Tuanshan Hill, giving visitors a chance to stop and mingle with the friendly lake folk.

Erhai Lake

The great Erhai, blessing and bane of the Dali Plain, is a constant fixture in the consciousness of the Bai people. It is deep and full of fish. Predictable winds blow from the north in the morning and change direction at day's end, filling the sails of the wooden boats transporting quarry stones, fish, livestock, fodder or wood around the shores. But the lake has another face that is far less benign. Heavy rains can bring devastating floods. Today, dams and predictions from provincial weather stations help to avert disasters.

There are innumerable ways to enjoy the lake — walking along the shore or hiring boats to explore islands and inlets. Keep in mind that the waters are infested with the schistosomiasis worm and therefore it is unsafe to swim.

Boats are easily come by. Regular excursions by launch are arranged by CITS; departure times can be found at the Erhai Guesthouse. Launches leave from the waterfront along Binhe Nan Lu, where the Xi'er River flows from the lake. These large pleasure boats, capable of holding 100 or more people, can be chartered by groups for Rmb360 for a whole day, or Rmb200 for five hours. Many types of fishing and transport boats gather along the waterfront as well, if you want to hire one privately. You will have to bargain over the price. A rule of thumb might be Rmb20 for half a day, but if you speak some Chinese you could undoubtedly do better.

There are three main islands and several temples and villages along the lake's dry eastern shore that are worth visiting. About an hour by boat from Xiaguan is **Golden Shuttle Island** (Jinsuo Dao), with a small fishing community on the east side and a cave for exploring. On the shore, directly north of the island, is a rocky peninsula crowned by a pavilion and temple. Sacred Buddhist buildings, destroyed and rebuilt many times, have stood on this spot for nearly 1,500 years. Luoquan Temple was badly damaged during the Cultural Revolution but is slowly being put back together and has great charm. Visitors can have their fortunes told by an old priest who guides them in shaking and selecting a single bamboo stick from a bundle of 100. The numbered stick corresponds to a specific fortune.

Much farther up the lake sits a tiny, picturesque temple island, **Xiao Putuo Dao**, dating from the 15th century. It is devoted to Guanyin, the Goddess of Mercy. The outside walls have been restored with paintings of birds, animals and flowers and the fanciful roof with pointed eaves is especially nice. On the shore nearby is the fishing village of **Haiyin**, whose boatmen are steeped in the lore of the lake. One of their specialities is night fishing for the huge 40-kilo (88-pound) 'green fish'.

Approaching the northern end of Erhai is the village of **Tianshengyin** and the twin islets of **Chiwen Dao** and **Yuji Dao**, a beautiful grouping with old buildings and a pagoda. Sometimes it is possible to catch a boat

from here across the lake to Shangguan, near Butterfly Spring (see page 119), and then ride a bus home to Dali or Xiaguan.

Three Pagodas of Dali (Dali Santa)

Standing below Lanfeng Peak, slightly to the northwest of Dali Town, are three elegant pagodas, known as Chongsheng Santa, the Three Pagodas of Saintly Worship. The outstanding landmarks of the region, they were once part of the greatest temple complex on the Dali plain. The Chongsheng Temple itself has long since disappeared and now only the towers remain.

The tallest pagoda, named Qianxunta, measures 70 metres (230 feet). It was constructed in the middle of the ninth century under the guidance of three engineers from Chang'an (modern Xi'an), capital of the Tang Dynasty. It has 16 tiers. The two smaller pagodas, each with ten tiers and standing 42 metres (135 feet) high, were built 200 years later.

Pagodas are among the most ubiquitous structures throughout the Buddhist world. Their Sanskrit name is stupa, originally a round dome or cylinder on a square base with a shaft emerging upward.

Stupas probably evolved in India from prehistoric times as burial mounds for local rulers and heroes. Legend says that in the fifth century BC Sakyamuni, the historical Buddha, asked to have his ashes interred in a stupa. Since that time stupas have become symbols of the Buddha, reminders of his earthly existence, cult objects and places of devotion.

As Buddhism spread through Asia the shape of stupas adapted itself to local architecture, giving rise to the huge variety of styles. Generally speaking there are three types of stupas, or pagodas, in China.

The storeyed style This results from traditional Chinese storeyed architecture and is marked by panoramic views from large windows and outer railings at each level.

The pavilion style This is also known as the 'single-layered stupa', with one storey only.

The close-eaves style These pagodas are characterized by a spacious first storey, low subsequent storeys and all eaves spaced closely to one another. Windows are small or non-existent and the interior space is cramped and dark. Close-eaves pagodas are an early style whose popularity rested on the extreme simplicity and gracefulness of form. They are best viewed from a distance where their lines can be seen in relief against a mountain or the far horizon.

The Chongsheng Santa are clearly of the third type, as are nearly all remaining pagodas on the Dali plain. They were built by the 'earth stacking method', whereby terraces of earth were constructed around the pagoda as it rose storey by storey. The immense outer structure of dirt was finally removed to reveal the finished masterpiece.

The pagodas were founded for two main reasons. First, they were holy

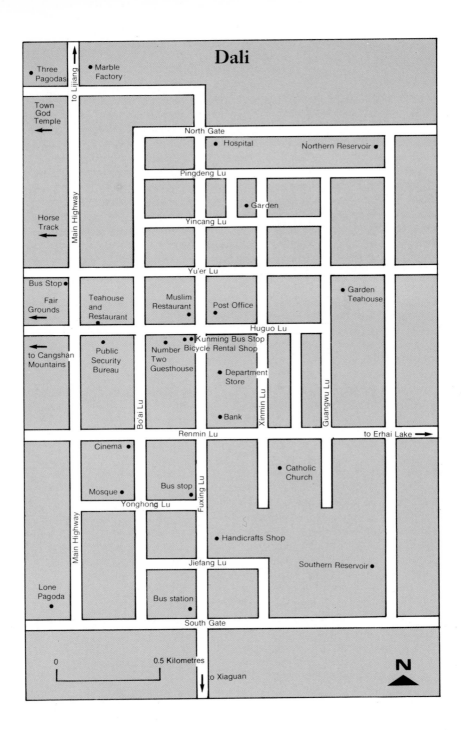

structures that invoked the Buddha's protection against the frequent
disasters of floods and earthquakes. A carved marble inscription in front of
Qianxunta bears the four Chinese characters *yong zhen shan chuan*, Subdue
Forever the Mountains and the Rivers. Secondly, the pagodas were re-
liquaries for the ashes and bones of saints and a storehouse for scriptures
and precious objects. During reconstruction work in 1979 a priceless
hoard, of paintings, sutras, jewels, unguents and medicines, copper
mirrors, gold and silver ornaments, utensils and musical instruments was
discovered. A small museum behind the pagodas recounts their history.

Dali Marble Factory (Dalishichang)

There are over 30 marble factories throughout China but this is the most
famous. Small wonder considering the Chinese word for marble is *dalishi*
(Dali stone). Marble of the finest quality has been quarried here for 1,200
years and the great scars high up on the faces of Cangshan have only begun
to eat into a supply that will last for millennia.

The factory on the northern outskirts of Dali was set up in 1956 and
most of its 180 employees have ancestors who were marble workers.
Products are made from a choice of four kinds of marble: 'pure white',
'coloured flower', 'cloud grey' and 'handicraft marble'. It is fascinating to
see giant slicing machines slowly cutting through five-ton blocks of marble,
a process that takes two or three days. Each year 6,000 square metres
(7,200 square yards) of marble are prepared and most of it is sent to
Guangzhou (Canton) for export to Hong Kong, Japan and Southeast Asia.

Marble carvings and statuary abound throughout the markets of Dali,
though most of the wares are not to the taste of foreigners, being either too
kitsch or too heavy. With time and a discerning eye, however, some really
worthy marble objects can be found. Thinly sliced discs or fan-shaped
pieces of marble, polished but uncarved, sometimes have a natural grain
resembling a classical Chinese mountain landscape.

Nanzhao Stele (Nanzhao Dehua Bei)

The Nanzhao Stele, also known by its formal name of Nanzhao Dehua Bei
(Nanzhao Sinicization Stele), is an historically important stone tablet from
the year 766. It records the offices of a bureaucracy under the Nanzhao
Kingdom, describes the economic and political system and specifies the
distribution of people within the realm. More important, it recounts
Nanzhao's on-off alliances with the Tang Dynasty.

The stele, a time-pocked black monolith 3 metres (10 feet) tall, stands
in a pavilion half way between Dali and Xiaguan on the rising slopes of the
plain, above the main road. It is between the Cangshan Range's Shengying
and Foding Peaks. This site was formerly within the city walls of Taihe,

Nanzhao's first capital. The Old Nanzhao Highway can still be seen nearby as a shallow furrow running away to the north.

The Nanzhao Stele was accidentally rediscovered and studied by a Qing-Dynasty scholar at the end of the 18th century. Were it not for him, the carved characters and the history they tell would have been lost. Much of the writing has indeed been obliterated, worn away by time and pilfered through the centuries by people seeking pieces of the stele to grind into powder for medicine.

Snake Bone Pagoda (Sheguta)

The dragon, one of China's most complex mythological symbols, has one manifestation whereby it rules over springs, lakes and water courses. Dragons were frequently blamed for the flooding of Erhai Lake and pagodas were erected for protection from the scaly monsters. Snake Bone Pagoda was built to commemorate a brave young man who died while vanquishing one of these 'dragons', which in fact turned out to be a large python, a perfect surrogate and scapegoat. The common people burned the devil snake and buried its bones under the pagoda.

Snake Bone Pagoda is similar in form to Qianxunta, stands 39 metres (128 feet) tall and was built at the end of the ninth century. It is located under Xieyang Peak 4 kilometres (2.5 miles) northwest of Xiaguan.

Butterfly Spring (Hudiequan)

This prosaic site in no way approaches its high reputation, but by hiking under the last of Cangshan's 19 peaks and exploring the northern end of Erhai Lake, a visit here can be turned to good advantage.

The legend of Butterfly Spring tells how this spot was a tryst for two young lovers of the Bai nationality. They were happy beyond words but, tragically, hidebound social rules, inflexible elders and persecution drove them to a double suicide. Ever since, they have re-emerged each spring as a pair of butterflies, accompanied by their mascot companion, a golden deer, which now appears as a small, yellow butterfly.

The spring, in a shady grove on the lower slopes of the Cangshan, was justifiably famous for centuries because of a breathtaking convergence every springtime of tens of thousands of butterflies to this spot. The phenomenon was documented many times. Alas, since the mass introduction of insecticides in 1958 the numbers have steadily diminished and the spectacle no longer occurs.

Butterfly Spring lies just off the main road, 35 kilometres (22 miles) north of Dali. The spring itself forms a clear pool and the hills above afford a fine view of the lake.

Zhoucheng and Xizhou Villages

These two villages, containing some first-rate architecture, still carry on the unspoilt daily rhythm of life on the Dali plain.

Zhoucheng Village lies near Butterfly Spring, 30 kilometres (19 miles) north of Dali on the main road. Its inhabitants are nearly pure Bai, with only 50 of its 1,500 households belonging to non-Bai people (Han, Naxi and Dai). Zhoucheng rests below Yunlong Peak and has achieved considerable wealth through its dynamic agriculture and diversified cottage industries. In recent years the locals have set about producing confectionery, noodles, liquor, toys and tie-dyed cloth. There is a boom in house building as well. The solid construction, attention to detail, roofing and stone masonry are all impressive.

Two giant fig trees (*Ficus stipulata*) stand in the main market square, a place where young and old gather to buy and sell produce, meet with friends, swap stories and enjoy themselves. Every Bai village tries to maintain such trees for beauty, shade and blessing.

Xizhou Village has a more mixed population and cosmopolitan background. It grew and flourished in the Ming Dynasty (1368−1644) along with the fortunes of Dali's renowned tea merchants. Each year enormous trains of pack animals would set out from Xiaguan loaded with bricks of tea for the thirsty markets of Tibet. This lucrative trade spawned a class of financiers and agents who in time gathered in Xizhou to build their gardens and pleasure-houses. Although sadly run-down, many of these eccentric structures remain, including a French *fin de siècle* mansion.

Xizhou is also famous for producing carved doors and staircases, which can be seen for sale on market days up and down the Dali plain. The village lies 3 kilometres (1.8 miles) east of the main north-south road; the turn-off is 20 kilometres (12.5 miles) north of Dali, just before the bridge over Wanhua Stream. Farther down a side road beyond Xizhou lies the protected port of Haishe in a serene lakeside setting of spits, promontories, islets and inlets.

Other Sights

The Dali Plain, with a long and florid history, is dotted here and there with miscellaneous cultural sites and tumbledown ruins. Listed below are some less well-known places that can form part of a day trip from either Xiaguan or Dali.

Around Xiaguan are the **Confucius Temple, Han Dynasty Tomb, Wanren Tomb** and **Gantong Temple**. Slightly to the northwest lies **Jiangjun Temple**, erected to honour General Limi, a Tang emissary who suppressed the Dali Kingdom (936−1253).

The **Dali city wall** and **gate tower** were built during the Ming

Dynasty (1368–1644). The gate tower, known as the Tower of Five Glories, was one of the finest in all China, far outshining in splendour the present 1984 reconstruction.

Near Dali, beyond the southwest corner of the town, is **Lone Pagoda** (Yita), a close-eaves style pagoda built during the tenth century. Farther down the plain, below Zhong He Peak, stand the remains of the **Kublai Khan Memorial Stele**, a huge 4.4-metre (14-foot) inscribed stone mounted on an enormous turtle. Two styles of calligraphy were used to praise Kublai Khan's conquest of Dali in 1253. The date of the inscription is not known. The small **Goddess of Mercy Temple** (Guanyintang) lies 5 kilometres (3 miles) south of Dali. It is built over a great rock which, legend says, was brought there by the goddess herself to block the path of an invading army. At the far northern end of Erhai Lake, beyond Butterfly Spring, lies the village of **Shaping**, host to a lively, colourful market each Monday. There is a small hotel here. Boats from Caicun to **Wase** on the eastern shore leave each day at approximately 3 pm. Wase has a guesthouse, and a market every Saturday. **Shuanglang**, at the far northeast end of Erhai Lake, is a bucolic village with a Sunday market.

Sights beyond Dali

Chicken Foot Mountain (Jizushan)

Northeast of Dali in Binchuan County stands Jizushan, a high, sacred mountain that rises 3,220 metres (10,562 feet). It has been an important pilgrimage site and monastic centre for both Buddhists and Daoists since the seventh century. The mountain gets its peculiar name from the ridges that run across its face from west to southeast in the shape of a giant chicken's foot. It can be reached by taking a bus from Xiaguan to Binchuan, a distance of 70 kilometres (44 miles), and then carrying on another 24 kilometres (15 miles) to the Bai village of Shazhi at Jizushan's base.

For energetic hikers, the long walk up is amply rewarded by the view from the summit. The mountain's isolation and splendid position between Erhai Lake and the upper reaches of the Yangzi River have frequently been praised by poets:

> Sunrise in the East
> Cangshan's nineteen peaks in the West
> Snow to the North
> Endless hills and clouds to the South

This holy mountain, once alive with over 360 temples and hermitages, was systematically attacked by Red Guards in the late 1960s, purportedly to end 'superstition, alchemy and madness'. Every major site was damaged or destroyed and only now, 20 years later, are the pieces being put back to-

Logging is a major industry in many parts of Yunnan. Here in the northwest, loggers gather at a roadhead to begin loading timber onto trucks for the long, four-day trip to Kunming.

gether. Even so it is impossible to hope or imagine that Jizushan will ever come close to recreating its formidable past when representatives from Buddhist countries all over Asia came there to live. Weather-beaten Tibetans arrived regularly after travelling the pilgrim road for months or years. On this mountain the diverse theologies of Hinayana, Mahayana and Lamaistic Buddhism mingled freely in one place.

Sacred Wish (Zhusheng) was the central temple on the mountain. It honoured the monk Jiaye who came from India to spread Buddhism. Legend recounts how Jiaye established Buddhism on Jizushan by mastering magical forces and overcoming the wicked Chicken Foot King in titanic battles. Zhusheng Temple was renowned for its bronze statuary and two enormous brass cauldrons, each capable of holding enough rice to feed 1,000 people.

The climb up the mountain leads through remnants of famous walnut forests that once supplied Dali with house beams and wood for the coffins of the rich. The top of the mountain is called Heavenly Pillar Peak (Tian-zhu Feng) and nearby on a precipice is the crowning spire, Lengyan Pagoda. It is a square, close-eaves style pagoda that rises 40 metres (130 feet). It was built between 650−655 and has remained the symbol of Jizu-shan despite all the devastation.

Stone Bell Mountain Buddhist Caves (Shizhongshan Shiku)

China is rich in Buddhist cave centres; most notable amongst these are Bezeklik and Kizil in Xinjiang, Dunhuang and Maijishan in Gansu Province, Yungang in Shanxi Province, Longmen in Henan Province and Dazu in Sichuan Province. The Stone Bell Mountain Caves, though less extensive than these, are Yunnan's finest, a complex of three main sites carved and constructed between the years 649−1094. They are in a remote mountain region 130 kilometres (81 miles) north of Dali by road in Jian-chuan County. Follow the main highway towards Lijiang as far as the village of Diannan, 8 kilometres (5 miles) before Jianchuan. There is a complicated intersection here. As you turn left (west), be sure to stay on the road that angles back towards the southwest. Do not go in the direction of Yangling. Rather, follow the southwest road for 24 kilometres (15 miles). You will find the caves before reaching the village of Shaxi. Sixteen grottoes have been discovered, shared between the sites of **Stone Bell Mountain Temple**, **Lion Pass** (Shiziguan), and **Shadeng Village**, which are all in the same vicinity. Most of the grottoes are at Shadeng.

Apart from the expected pantheon of Buddhist deities and disciples and scenes from the life of the Buddha (Jattaka Tales), these caves are outstanding for their presentation of life under the Nanzhao Kingdom. The works are mostly carvings, with some frescoes, too. Depictions of foreigners with aquiline noses, beards and high brows indicate contacts through trade and diplomacy. Habits, clothing and customs of the Nanzhao royal family are shown in vivid detail; Grotto Number One at Stone Bell Mountain holds nine imperial figures with one seated amidst the others wearing a long, elaborate gown. This is King Yi Mouxun (reigned 779 – 808), under whose rule Nanzhao increasingly adopted Tang models for political institutions, and borrowed Chinese cultural and literary forms.

Another cave at Stone Bell Mountain is known as the Ge Luofeng Grotto. Ge Luofeng was a Nanzhao king as well, 30 years before Yi Mouxun. During his reign Nanzhao forces dealt the Tang armies a series of crushing defeats. This grotto is carefully carved to give the impression of a resplendent hall, with three overlapping tiers carved into the perimeter of the cave. Inside at the centre sits the solemn king, surrounded by dogs, courtiers, soldiers, ministers and an influential monk, all in full regalia.

Certainly the most extraordinary cave is the Grotto of Female Genitalia. Here artists have carried the praise and veneration of fertility to an amazing degree, with graphic depictions and an imaginary man-high vagina.

This cave and the possible embarrassment it might bring to tourists and tour guides alike is one reason why the Stone Bell Mountain complex has been closed for so long. But the official line has changed and, as the Chinese now say, 'these are important cultural relics for research work, for in-depth investigations into Nanzhao social life'.

Rainbow Bridge (Jihongqiao)

This iron chain bridge crosses a deep gorge of the Mekong River (Lancang Jiang) 185 kilometres (115 miles) by road southwest from Xiaguan. Special permission from CITS and at least a week's advance notice are needed in order to make this trip. Rainbow Bridge is reached by first going westward to Yongping, then travelling southward for 38 kilometres (24 miles) to Changjie (Changgai). After this, continue westward again for 20 kilometres (12.5 miles) to Yonghe and then on to the river.

Although records show iron bridges to have existed in this part of the world since the Eastern Han Dynasty (AD 25 – 200), Rainbow Bridge is the only one with a continuous history of a thousand years in one location. The bridge we see today was built in 1475 and consists of 17 iron chains, each chain made up of 176 rings. The length is 60 metres (197 feet) and the width 3.8 metres (12.5 feet). Wooden boards are laid across the chains to allow people and animals to cross, a risky proposal because of the bridge's dilapidated condition.

Pavilions and poems carved in the surrounding cliffs attest to the importance of Rainbow Bridge as a vital trade and diplomatic link with India, Burma and Thailand. Distinguished tourists of the past have visited here, including Emperor Kangxi (reigned 1661 – 1722) and Marco Polo.

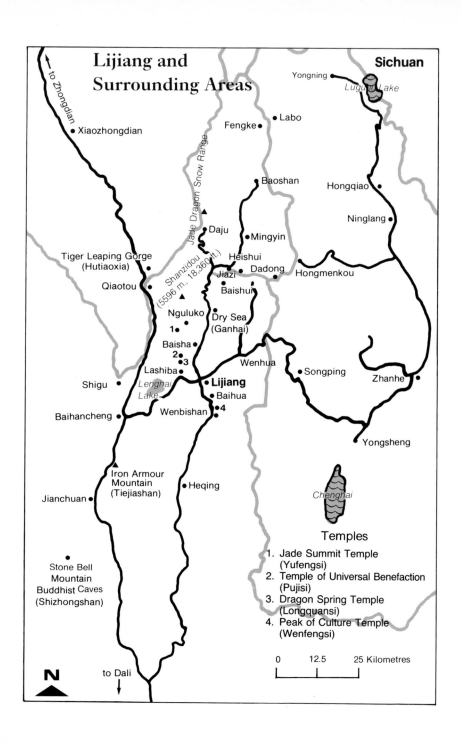

Lijiang and Surrounding Areas

Sichuan

to Zhongdian

Yongning

Lugu Lake

Xiaozhongdian

Fengke

Labo

Jade Dragon Snow Range

Baoshan

Hongqiao

Ninglang

Daju

Mingyin

Tiger Leaping Gorge
(Hutiaoxia)

Shanzidou
(5596 m., 18,360 ft.)

Heishui

Dadong

Hongmenkou

Qiaotou

Jiazi

Baishui

Nguluko

Dry Sea
(Ganhai)

1

Baisha

2

3

Lashiba

Wenhua

Songping

Zhanhe

Shigu

Lenghai
Lake

Lijiang

Baihua

Baihancheng

Wenbishan

4

Yongsheng

Iron Armour
Mountain
(Tiejiashan)

Heqing

Chenghai

Jianchuan

Stone Bell
Mountain
Buddhist Caves
(Shizhongshan)

Temples

1. Jade Summit Temple
   (Yufengsi)
2. Temple of Universal Benefaction
   (Pujisi)
3. Dragon Spring Temple
   (Longquansi)
4. Peak of Culture Temple
   (Wenfengsi)

N

to Dali

0   12.5   25 Kilometres

Lijiang

The remote town of Lijiang is the centre of the Naxi people, a small (250,000) matriarchal tribe with a richly textured culture. Lijiang, nestled in a broad, fertile valley, is divided by Lion Hill into two distinct parts. New Lijiang, only 35 years old, is an uninspiring, cement clone of innumerable modern Chinese cities. It could not be more different from Old Lijiang, an intimate mountain town of stone and tile, laced with swift canals. Dominating the valley, the snowy heads of the Jade Dragon Snow Range (Yulongxueshan) make a craggy pile of 13 peaks, a sharp contrast to the long, looping skyline of Dali's Cangshan.

Old Lijiang has supported a stable population of 50,000 people for most of its 800 years. It is a gathering place of rugged mountain people from various ethnic groups with names such as Lisu, Pumi and Nuosu Yi, but the majority are Naxi. New Lijiang, populated largely by Han Chinese, is growing and encroaching on the old city.

The origin of the Naxi, like many of China's minority groups, is not fully known. Most scholars agree, however, that there was a proto-ethnic tribe, the Qiang, who dwelt in the mountains of northwestern China (today's Qinghai, Gansu and Sichuan Provinces) several thousand years ago. Northern invaders drove them south where they splintered into individual tribes. The Naxi are one of these; they speak a Tibeto-Burman language of their own.

The Naxi themselves believe they came from a common ancestor named Tabu who helped them hatch from magic eggs. Their creation myth is depicted in booklets made of resilient, insect-proof bark dating probably from the tenth century. Shamans, called *dongbas*, were the only people who could read and write the unique Naxi picture-script. Dongbas have vanished as a functioning element in modern Naxi society, but a major effort is under way to preserve their wisdom and lore.

One characteristic that strikes the visitor is the predominance of women in all types of work. Matriarchal in their social structure (inheritance passes through the youngest daughter), women run the market and control the purse-strings. Although men are by no means indolent, they were traditionally gardeners, child-rearers and musicians. In recent years there has been a remarkable resurgence of traditional music, an ancient legacy the Naxi have kept alive since Kublai Khan's invasion in the 13th century. Twenty-two compositions remain from the original repertoire, with sweet, peaceful names such as 'Wind from the River', 'Summer has Come', 'Ten Gifts from God' and 'The Water Dragon is Singing'. At least four full orchestras of elderly men have formed in and around Lijiang. The old instruments are thrilling to see; a weathered transverse flute, a copper gong-frame, Chinese lutes, three-stringed 'banjos', enormous cymbals, a wooden fish-shaped drum. Every visitor should try to spend an evening listening to the marvellous, slow, lilting music.

Men have also always had time to indulge their passion for horses. Lijiang is still known by the nickname Land of Horses. Horses and mules are the focus of two animal fairs every April and September, reminders of grander days when Lijiang formed one end of Tibet's caravan route between India and China. The Naxi acted as middlemen, and at times a quarter of Lijiang's population was made up of Tibetan traders. Modern roads and trucks have bypassed Lijiang. Robbed of their old role, the practical Naxi now profit from their abundant forests which they harvest for timber-hungry China.

The Naxi people have had a long history of interaction with the Chinese and today, under the irresistible force of modernization, contacts are increasing and ways of life are changing. Nevertheless, the Naxi hold fast to their cultural roots and in the inaccessible hinterland to the north old customs continue virtually untouched by the outside world.

In Lijiang: Rock's Kingdom

Bruce Chatwin

It is a cold, sunny Sunday in Yunnan. On the plain below Jade Dragon Mountain, the villagers of Baisha are letting off fire-crackers to celebrate the building of a house, and the village doctor is holding a feast in his upper room, in honour of his firstborn grandson.

The sun filters through the lattices, bounces off rafters hung with corn-cobs and lights up everyone's faces. Apart from us, almost all the guests are members of the Naxi (Nakhi) tribe.

The Naxi are the descendants of Tibetan nomads who, many centuries ago, exchanged their tents for houses and settled in the Lijiang Valley, to grow rice and buckwheat at an altitude of over 8,000 feet. Their religion was — and surreptitiously still is — a combination of Tibetan Lamaism, Chinese Daoism and a far, far older shamanistic belief: in the spirits of cloud and wind and pine.

The Doctor has seated us, with his four brothers, at the table of honour beside the east window.

Below, along the street, there are lines of weeping willows and a quick-water stream in which some pale brown ducks are playing. Led by the drake, they swim furiously against the current, whiz back down to the bridge and then begin all over again.

The panelled housefronts are painted the colour of ox blood. Their walls are of mud brick, flecked with chaff, and their tiled roofs stretch away, rising and sagging, in the direction of the old dynastic temple of the ancient kings of Mu.

None of the Doctor's brothers look the least bit alike. The most vigorous is a leathery, Mongol-eyed peasant, who keeps refilling my bowl of firewater. The second, with bristly grey hair and a face of smiling wrinkles, sits immobile as a meditating monk. The other two are a tiny man with a wandering gaze and a shadowy presence under a fur-lined hat.

Looking across to the ladies' table, we are amazed by the fullfleshed, dimpled beauty of the young girls and the quiet dignity of the older women. They are all in traditional costume, in the celestial colours — blue and white. Some, it is true, are wearing Mao caps, but most are in a curved blue bonnet, rather like a Flemish coif. Our Shanghai friend, Tsong-Zung, says we might well be guests at Bruegel's 'Peasant Wedding'.

Apart from the bonnet, the women's costume consists of a blue bodice, a pleated white apron and a stiff, quilted cape secured with crossbands. Every Naxi woman carries the cosmos on her back: the upper part of the cape is a band of indigo representing the night sky; the lower, a lobe of creamy silk or sheepskin that stands for the light of day. The two halves are separated by a row of seven disks that symbolize the stars — although the sun and moon, once worn on either shoulder, have now gone out of fashion.

Girls come up from the kitchen with the sweet course: apples preserved in honey, melon in ginger, sour plums in alcohol. More girls then come with the Nine Dishes — the Nine Dragons, as they've been called since the Zhou (Chou) Dynasty: in this case, cubes of pork fat and winter sausage, water chestnuts, lotus root, carp, taros, bean tops, rice fritters, a fungus known as tree ears, and a heap of tripe and antique eggs that go, like sulphur bombs, straight to the gut.

From time to time, the Doctor himself appears at the head of the stairs, in a white clinician's mobcap and silver-grey cotton greatcoat. He surveys the company with the amused, slightly otherworldly air of a Daoist gentleman-scholar, and flicks his wispy beard from side to side. As soon as the meal is over, he appears again, hypodermic in hand, as if to remind us that healing, even on the 'Big Happy Day', is a work without end.

The grandson's name is Deshou: 'De' for virtue, 'Shou' for longevity. On a sheet of red paper, now pinned to the porch, the old man has written the following:

The grandfather grants his grandson the name 'Deshou'.
De is high as the Big Dipper.
Shou is like the southern mountain.
De is valued by the world.
Shou respected by men.
De is an oily rain.
Shou the fertilized field.
Long life and health to him, born 10.30 am, 9th Moon, 14th Day.

The focus of all this adoration is swaddled in a length of gold-and-purple Tibetan brocade, and has the face of a man born wise. He is on show downstairs, in his mother's lap. The bedroom has white-papered walls to which are pasted scarlet cut-outs of characters representing happiness and of butterflies flying in pairs.

Apart from the Doctor's herbal and his English dictionary, the swaddling clothes are the family's only treasure to survive the Cultural Revolution, when Red Guards ransacked the house.

The Doctor takes the baby and cradles him in his arms.

'I have plenty,' he says, gesturing to the revellers in the courtyard. 'Six years ago I had nothing. But now I have plenty.' His wife comes from the kitchen and stands beside him. And with her deep blue bonnet, and smile of tender resignation, she reminds us of Martha or Mary in a Florentine altarpiece.

The Red Guards stripped him of everything, and he was forbidden to practise. 'It was she who saved me,' he says. 'Without her I could not have lived.'

Their son, the father of three weeks' standing, is a young man of 27 in a neat blue Chinese suit. He is a self-taught teacher of English, and now also a student of medicine.

Proudly, he shows us his wedding cup — a porcelain bowl painted with peacocks, on which the village calligrapher has added a couplet by the Tang poet Bai Juyi:

One only wishes that people will live forever
And be in couples even at a distance of 1,000 *li*

The calligraher — a courteous, hook-nosed old gentleman — is the Doctor's cousin and also one of the party. He has spent many years, as an ideological bygone, in jail. But now — in this new, relaxed, undoctrinaire China — he has retired to his tiny house by the stream: to practise the arts of seal cutting, brush-work and the culture of orchids. On Tuesday, when we called on him, he showed us a lilac autumn crocus, with a label in Chinese reading 'Italian autumn narcissus'.

The Doctor, too, is a passionate plant collector, though of a rather different stamp. Behind his surgery is a garden with paths of pebblemosaic where a plum tree casts its shadow, like a sundial, on the whitewashed walls, and there are raised beds for growing medicinal herbs. Most of the herbs he has gathered himself, from the slopes of the Snow Range: heaven's hemp (for the bladder); orchid root (for migraine); *Meconopsis horridula* (for dysentery); and a lichen that will cure shrunken ovaries, or bronchitis if taken with bear's grease.

He owes much of his botanical knowledge to his student days in Nanjing. But some he learned from the strange, solitary European — with red face, spectacles and a terrible temper — who taught him his first smattering of English; at whom, as his retinue passed up the village street, the boys would clamour: 'Le-Ke! Le-Ke!' — 'Rock! Rock!' — and scamper out of reach.

Joseph F. Rock — 'Dr. Lock' as the Naxi remember him — was the Austro-American botanist and explorer who lived in the Lijiang Valley, off and on from 1922 to 1949. He is our excuse for coming here. My interest in him goes back many years to a summer evening in the Arnold Arboretum in Boston, when I found that all the trees I liked best bore Rock's name on their labels.

'Tell me,' the Doctor asked on a previous visit, 'Why was Le-Ke so angry with us?'

'He wasn't angry with you,' I said. 'He was born angry.'

I should perhaps have added that the targets of his anger included the National Geographic magazine (for rewriting his prose), his Viennese nephew, Harvard University, women, the State Department, the Guomindang, Reds, red tape, missionaries, Holy Rollers, Chinese bandits and bankrupt Western civilization.

Rock was the son of an Austrian manservant who ended up as major-domo to a Polish nobleman, Count Potocki. His mother died when he was six. At 13, already under the spell of an imaginary Cathay, he taught himself Chinese characters. I like to think that, from the library of his father's employer, he read, and acted on, Count Potocki's novel of aristocrats in far-flung places: 'The Saragossa Manuscript'.

Tuberculosis notwithstanding, young Rock ran away to sea: to Hamburg, to New York, to Honolulu — where, without training, he set himself up as the botanist of the Hawaiian Islands. He wrote three indispensable books on the flora, then went to Burma in search of a plant to cure leprosy. He 'discovered' Lijiang, thereafter to be the base for his travels along the Tibetan border: to the former kingdoms of Muli, Choni and Yungning, and to the mountain of Minya Konka, which, in a moment of rashness, he claimed to be the highest in the world. (He had miscalculated by about a mile.) Yet, though he introduced hundreds of new or rare plants to Western gardens and sent off thousands and thousands of herbarium specimens, he never wrote a paper on the botany of China.

Instead, he gave his life to recording the customs, ceremonies and the unique pictographic script of his Naxi friends. Lijiang was the only home he ever knew; and after he was booted out, he could still write, in a letter, 'I want to die among those beautiful mountains rather than in a bleak hospital bed all alone.'

This, then, was the meticulous autodidact, who would pack *David Copperfield* in his baggage to remind him of his wretched childhood; who travelled 'en prince' (at the expense of his American backers), ate off gold plate, played records of Caruso to mountain villagers and liked to glance back, across a hillside, at his cavalcade 'half a mile long'.

His book *The Ancient Nakhi Kingdom of South-West China*, with its eye-aching genealogies and dazzling asides, must be one of the most eccentric publications ever produced by the Harvard University Press.

Here is a stretch of his embattled prose: 'A short distance beyond, at a tiny temple, the trail ascends the red hills covered with oaks, pines, *Pinus armandi*, *P. yunnanensis*, Alnus, *Castanopsis delavayi*, rhododendrons, roses, berberis, etc., up over limestone mountains, through oak forest, to a pass with a few houses called Ch'ou-shui-ching (Stinking water will). At this place many hold-ups and murders were committed by the bandit hordes of Chang Chiehpa. He strung up his victims by the thumbs to the branches of high trees, and tied rocks to their feet; lighting a fire beneath he left them to their fate. It was always a dreaded pass for caravans. At the summit there are large groves of oaks (*Quercus delavayi*). . . .'

No wonder Ezra Pound adored it!

Pound appears to have got hold of Rock's *Nakhi Kingdom* in 1956, at a time when he was locked up as a lunatic in St. Elizabeth's Hospital in Washington; from it, he extrapolated the upland paradise that was to be, in effect, his lifeline.

Over the last week we have been walking the roads of Lijiang country and finding, to our delight, that the world Rock 'saved us for memory' — to say nothing of Ezra Pound's borrowings — is very far from dead.

At Rock's former lodgings in Lijiang town, we have seen his bookcase, his pigeonhole desk, his wide chair ('because he was so fat!') and the remains of his garden beside the Jade Stream.

At Nuluko (the name means 'the foot of the silver cliffs') his country house is almost as he left it, except that, instead of herbarium specimens, the porch is spread with drying turnip tops. The present occupant, Li Wenbiao, was one of Rock's muleteers; he showed us the master's camp bed and the washhouse where he would set up a canvas bath from Abercrombie & Fitch.

We have been to Tiger Leaping Gorge and seen the cliff line plummeting 11,000 feet into the Yangzi. We have watched the Naxi women coming down from the Snow Range, with their bundles of pine and artemisia; and one old woman with a bamboo winnowing basket on her back, and the sun's rays passing through it:

Artemisia
Arundinaria
Winnowed in fate's tray. . .
       — 'Canto CXII'

The wild pear trees are scarlet in the foothills, the larches like golden pagodas; the north slopes 'blue-green with juniper'. The last of the gentians are in flower, and flocks of black sheep brindle the plain.

When the stag drinks at the salt spring
and sheep come down with the gentian sprout, . . .
       — 'Canto CXII'

One evening, walking back to town across the fields, I came on a boy and

girl reading aloud beside the embers of a fire. Their book was a traditional Chinese romance and, on its open page, there was a picture of Guanyin, Goddess of Mercy.

The Naxi are a passionate people, and even today, rather than submit to a hated marriage, young lovers may poison or drown themselves, or jump to their death from the mountain.

At the Naxi Institute in Lijiang, we were shown a pair of pine saplings, adorned like Christmas trees, commemorating two people who killed themselves for love. Rock wrote that such suicides become 'windspirits', reminding Pound of Dante's Paolo and Francesca, whose shades were 'so light on the wind,' and who, readers of the *Inferno* will remember, fell in love while reading a romance of chivalry.

At Shigu, where the Yangzi takes a hairpin bend, we have seen the Stone Drum:

> by the waters of Stone Drum,
> the two aces...
>   — 'Canto CI'

The drum is a cylinder of marble in a pavilion by the willows. The 'aces' refers to two Chinese generals — one lost in legend, the other of the Ming Dynasty, whose victory is recorded on the drum itself. Our friend Tzong-Zung raised his hand to the surface and rattled off the characters:

> Snowflakes the size of a hand
> Rain joining sunset to sunset
> The wind quick as arrows...
> Commands quick as lightning
> And the bandits loose their gall...
> Their black flag falls to the earth...
> They run for their lives...
> Heads heaped like grave mounds
> Blood like rain...
> The dikes choked with armour and rattan shields
> The trail of foxes and the trail of jackals
> Have vanished from the battlefield...

Rock wrote of a tradition that, should the Stone Drum split, a catastrophe will fall on the country. About 15 years ago, some Red Guards did, indeed, split it. (It has since been stuck together.) We wondered if, secretly, the iconoclasts had seen the foxes and jackals in themselves.

We have listened to a Naxi orchestra that in the bad years would practise in secret: on a stringless lute, a muffled drum and a flute turned at a right angle to the mouthpiece.

In the hills above Rock's village is the Jade Summit Monastery, Yufengsi, where we have sat with the lama hearing him tell how he would sneak into the monastery at night, on pain of prison or worse, to save the 500-year-old camellia that stretches, trained on a trellis, around the temple court.

Of all the places we have seen, the monastery seems the loveliest. But this
is what Rock had to say of it: 'It is the home of rats, whose excrements lie
inches deep. . . dangerous to visit. . . books wrapped in dusty silks. . . the most
forlorn and forsaken lamasery I know of.'

Also paying his respects to the lama was the Regional Commissioner for
Monuments. I asked him about the horribly battered temple, dating from the
Tang-dynasty, which we could see in the valley below. It is dedicated to the
mountain god, Saddo, lord of the Snow Range, and protector from
calamities.

The Commissioner answered, emphatically: 'The restoration will begin
next month,' as if also to say that the world's oldest, subtlest, most intelligent
civilization has now returned to the sources of its ancient wisdom.

In the village of Baisha, around the corner from the Doctor's house,
there is another, smaller temple, its garden desolate, its cypresses fallen, its
balustrades smeared with graffiti: 'Confess and we will be lenient!'

Here, under Daoist symbols of the Eternal Return, the Red Guards set
up their so-called courts. Yet it occurred to us that these ill-tempered scrawls
were not, after all, so distant from the spirit of the Daodejing (*Tao-te-ching*)
of Laozi (Lao-tze):

> How did the great rivers and seas gain dominion over the hundred lesser
> streams?
> By being lower than they.

The sun goes down behind the mountain, and we must, finally, say
goodbye to the Doctor. He is anxious to give me from his pharmacy a plant
with the windblown name of 'Saussurea gossipiphora', which only grows on
the snow line. Soon, he hopes to leave his practice in the care of his son and
be free to gather herbs in the mountains. He lifts his eyes to Jade Dragon
Peak and, suddenly, in his silver greatcoat, becomes the living image of my
favourite upland traveller, the poet Li Bo (as he appears in later pictures):

> You ask me why I live in the gray hills.
> I smile but do not answer, for my thoughts are elsewhere.
> Like peach petals carried by the stream, they have gone
> To other climates, to countries other than the world of men.

Bruce Chatwin is an eminent novelist and travel writer. His best-known books
include In Patagonia, On the Black Hill *and* The Viceroy of Ouidah.
This article first appeared in The New York Times Magazine (16 March 1986), as
In China: Rock's Kingdom.

Getting to Lijiang

Lijiang lies 196 kilometres (122 miles) north of Dali. The trip takes half a day by bus and as little as three hours by private car. Several buses leave from Xiaguan's main bus station each morning; some stop in Dali, others can be flagged down on the highway.

Traversing the Dali Plain at sunrise, cutting through the early morning mist, with the mountains and lake all around, is an unforgettable experience. The road starts to climb at Upper Gate (Shangguan), the strategically important town that has always guarded Dali's northern approach. Peaceful Erhai Lake is soon out of sight. **Jianchuan** is the first big town along the way, 136 kilometres (85 miles) from Xiaguan. On a clear day the bright, jagged peaks of Lijiang's Jade Dragon Snow Range can be seen on the northern horizon, whetting the traveller's anticipation. The important Buddhist cave site of Shizhongshan is southwest of Jianchuan. On the west side of the city is a small mountain called **Jinhuashan**. Half way up its slope the image of a Nanzhao general is carved on a cliff face, and nearby a sweet reclining Buddha whose rosy cheeks are created from two naturally formed red stones. Even farther west, on the banks of the Yongfeng River (Yongfenghe), stands the 18th-century **Longbaota**, a square, nine-tiered pagoda that rises 18 metres (59 feet). Its outstanding feature is the construction of small external shrines at each storey, with 32 Buddha images in every shrine.

Jianchuan is a county seat, predominantly Bai in make-up. It serves as a way station for buses. The town has a lively street market that occasionally produces remarkable items: ancient agricultural calendars; crude, hand-made jewellery; and old coins.

The dividing line between the Bai and the Naxi is a high ridge called **Iron Armour Mountain** (Tiejiashan). The road starts winding up it 24 kilometres (15 miles) after Jianchuan. Common lore, often borne out by observation, states that there is a preference for all things white south of Iron Armour Mountain, while to the north black is the favoured hue. For example, the Bai and Pumi minorities call themselves 'white', love bright colours and keep white sheep and goats. Beyond the mountain, the Naxi, Tibetans, Yi, and others favour black. Women's costumes are mainly black or dark blue and domesticated animals are black. Most of their names derive from roots meaning 'black'. The point should not be stretched too far, however.

The main north-south road in this part of Yunnan does not go directly to Lijiang; at Baihan Cheng a good paved road branches to the right. From here it is 45 kilometres (28 miles) to Lijiang, beginning with a long climb through azalea and rhododendron forests and including a wonderful straight section with an unobstructed view of the Jade Dragon Snow Range. The bus terminal is at the southwest edge of New Lijiang.

Hotel in Lijiang

Lijiang Guesthouse
(Lijiang Binguan)

丽江宾馆

This is the main hotel, located in New Lijiang across the street from the regional government offices, a 20-minute walk from the bus station. It has a new annex with 50 beds, mostly in simple, clean double rooms that cost Rmb20 per night. Rooms downstairs with three beds per room are cheaper. The walls and floors are made of wood and some of the double rooms have their own private bathroom with hot water at certain hours.

There is a dining room in the compound where foreigners can select from a good variety of moderately priced dishes. Be sure to check the price of the set meals beforehand.

The guesthouse has a small fleet of vehicles for hire — jeeps and a minibus. These are worth considering for long trips. Costs are in the area of Rmb1.50 per kilometre (Rmb2.4 per mile).

Food and Drink in Lijiang

Naxi cuisine may seem indelicate to a western gourmet; it depends on corn, wheat, beans and some rice, all of which conform to the short growing season. The main meat is pork and the Naxi love pork fat. The national dish is called *baba*. There is a Naxi ditty praising the bounty of the three big local towns: Heqing for wine, Jianchuan for pretty girls, Lijiang for *baba*. *Baba* is a thick, fried, wheat cake with every kind of filling: meat, onions, jam, melted sugar, honey, pork fat. A variation is *nuomi baba*, a smallish, chewy pancake of glutinous rice stuffed with something sweet. Some *babas* are really quite good and perfect for taking on picnics.

The Naxi make good wine which they drink from childhood. Honey Wine (*yin jiu*) is a smoky, nutty, honey-flavoured wine somewhat like sherry. Before the communist revolution of 1949 wine shops, run by women, abounded in towns, where men spent endless hours gossiping. *Yin jiu* is now bottled commercially, for local distribution, and can be bought at stalls throughout Lijiang.

Sights in the Lijiang Region

Black Dragon Pool (Heilongtan)

At the north end of town, directly under the steep slope of Elephant Hill, is Black Dragon Pool, the best known and most frequently visited park in

Lijiang. Walkways, willow and chestnut trees surround the pool itself, which has periodically gone dry in recent years, to the dismay of locals. Lijiang's classic picture-postcard view incorporates a willow, Black Dragon Pool, Moon-Embracing Pavilion (see below), and the towering snowy mountains as a backdrop. The view may be a cliché, but still there are several important buildings here.

The main entranceway is guarded by four stone lions that originally protected the Temple of Mu Tian Wang (see page 146), now destroyed. Passing through and going to the right, the first building is a library. It was brought to this site in 1982 from its original home at Fuguosi, where it was the second gate hall of that temple. Its reconstruction and repair have been well handled by an old Naxi artisan. The building possesses intricately joined, beautifully painted eaves.

The second building, just beyond the library, houses the Dongba Cultural Research Institute (see below).

Further along is **Dragon God Temple** (Longshenci), now turned into an exhibition hall for seasonal horticultural shows and art displays. It is a 17th-century structure with nice permanent gardens of forsythia, cherry and bonsai.

The most flamboyant structure within the park is **Five Phoenix Hall** (Wufenglou), built in the first years of the 17th century and moved *in toto* to this spot from Fuguosi between 1976 and 1979. Together with the library, Wufenglou is all that remains from the temple complex of Fuguosi 30 kilometres (19 miles) to the west, the oldest and formerly one of the most important Lamaist monasteries of Lijiang. This wooden building received the name Five Phoenix Hall from its exaggerated eaves; there are eight flaring roof points on each of the three storeys and an observer is always supposed to see at least five of these 'phoenixes' from any angle. There is a museum on the first floor, dusty and haphazardly kept, though filled with exotic and artistic gems. On display are clothes, head-dresses and swords of the *dongbas*, painted scrolls and *dongba* manuscripts, Tibetan prayer wheels and artifacts, along with charms, amulets and arcane shamanistic paraphernalia. Arrangements to see the museum should be made through the Dongba Institute.

Moon-Embracing Pavilion (Deyuelou) is the serene, beautifully proportioned structure that holds a place of honour next to Black Dragon Pool and the white marble Belt Bridge. The original three-storey pavilion dated from the late Ming Dynasty (1368–1644) and survived without significant damage until 1950. In that year, it is told with some glee, a high official took his paramour to Moon-Embracing Pavilion, where together they ate cakes and drank wine until the moon rose. Then the couple spread oil about, ignited it and offered themselves up in a spectacular double suicide, destroying the pavilion in the process. The present pavilion is a

The habitat of the yak lies between 4,000 and 6,000 metres (13,000 to 20,000 feet), though these long-haired oxen can work at lower altitudes for short periods of time. They provide transport, fuel in the form of dried dung, milk for butter and cheese, hair for felt and ropes, and hides for clothing. In northwestern Yunnan yaks are frequently used for hauling wood.

reconstruction from 1962. Belt Bridge, so named because it resembles a mandarin's belt, was also rebuilt after 1949.

Dongba Cultural Research Institute (Dongba Wenhua Yanjiushi)

Following the Chinese revolution of 1949, the folklore and history of the Naxi people might have been lost were it not for a few local scholars who started a small museum in 1954. The Yunnan Academy of Social Sciences incorporated it into a formal institute in 1981, the Dongba Cultural Research Institute. Its purpose is to study, document and preserve the ancient Naxi culture of the *dongbas*, religious shamans who played a pivotal role in traditional society. Only 30 or 40 *dongbas* are still alive, and five of these men are attached to the institute. Researchers are primarily engaged in the laborious work of translating thousands of *dongba jing* into Chinese. These small 'booklets', written in an archaic and bizarre script, are read aloud and taken down syllable by syllable; Naxi meaning and grammar are unscrambled and put into Chinese form and finally a proper translation is made. Needless to say, at this point very little deep investigation is being carried out in the intriguing fields of *dongba* religion, mythology, origination or history.

About a thousand of these booklets were written over the centuries, covering subjects ranging from accounting, through history and mythology, to exorcism and magic. Some 20,000 copies are scattered around the world. The Dongba Institute has approximately 5,000; the rest are in foreign university collections and a few in private hands. The goal of the Institute is to preserve, record, and ultimately produce an encyclopaedia of Naxi culture.

Five Main Temples of Lijiang (Lijiang Wuda Mingsi)

The 17th century was a great period of economic, political and cultural flowering in Lijiang. This renaissance is embodied in the life and works of Celestial King Mu (Mu Tian Wang), ruler from the ancient lineage of Naxi chiefs. Mu Tian Wang came to power in 1598 at the age of 11 and within two decades had chalked up a string of accomplishments that would be added to as his reign continued: poet and author, and an exemplary administrator who supervised large public works and enriched the entire region, he was appointed guardian of China's frontiers and pacified rebels and brigand tribes. The Ming Empire lavished deeds and titles upon him, built arches and town gates in his honour, and held up this non-Chinese as a model for other border peoples to emulate.

For all these worldly achievements, Mu Tian Wang was a deeply religious man who championed Buddhism through printing and publishing

Buddhist works and through the support of communities of monks. He had a direct hand in the construction of major temples around Lijiang and paid for the establishment of an important monastery on Chicken Foot Mountain (Jizushan).

His contributions were for the propagation of the Red Hat (Karmapa) sect of Tibetan Buddhism. The practices of this sect, dating from the mid-12th century, have always been closely bound up with the life of the common people, aiming not so much at theoretical knowledge as at its practical realization. Yoga and magic were frequently employed in Lijiang, on the wild border of Tibet, mixing with, and borrowing from, the *dongba* religion.

The main temples described below, patronized by Mu Tian Wang in the 17th century, are (or rather, were) all embodiments of the Karmapa sect.

Jade Summit Temple (Yufengsi) lies 11 kilometres (7 miles) northwest of Lijiang high up on a mountainside in the midst of pine woods, commanding a magnificent view over the valley. The group of buildings with white and grey tiled roofs is connected by stone steps and paths on several terraced levels. The first large hall on the left is the main Buddha hall, now badly damaged and acting as a friendly teahouse. It has remnants of Tibetan-style murals. To the right is a small cluster of enclosed buildings with a shrine containing a strange assortment of faded pictures. Yufengsi's sole lama resides here, shuffling around and happy to dress up in his old ecclesiastical robe at the mention of a photograph. The one superior building, at the highest level of the temple complex, deserves slow savouring. Its courtyard is laid out in beautiful geometric pebbled designs, doors and windows are finely carved, and in the middle, close to the entranceway, grows a remarkable centrepiece, an enormous and ancient camellia tree famous throughout Yunnan. Each year in late February or early March it unfailingly opens to display '20,000 blossoms'. Whether this number is actually correct becomes insignificant, in the face of such a *tour de force* of nature. Everyone far and wide cherishes this tree so it is essential to avoid Yufengsi on overcrowded Sundays.

Temple of Universal Benefaction (Pujisi) sits above the village of Pujicun, 5 kilometres (3 miles) northwest of Lijiang. From the plain it takes a half-hour climb through a maze of steep goat trails to reach the temple. Don't give up; local herdsmen will point you in the right direction. Two huge trees, Chinese flowering crabapple (*haitang*), stand within the courtyard. Beyond them is the Buddha hall, largely desecrated, but still containing murals, Buddha images and *thankas*, Tibetan painted scroll-banners presenting pictorial instruction on theology, astrology, and the lives of Buddhas, saints and deities. There are ruins above Pujisi that offer a fine view over the green and yellow fields far, far below.

The age-old 'rammed earth' method of building walls is employed in northwestern Yunnan. Workers use heavy, specially designed poles to pound earth between a frame of fixed boards. The earth rises higher and higher until finally the boards are removed to reveal the finished wall.

Peak of Culture Temple (Wenfengsi) lies under the unmistakeable landmark of Calligraphic Brush Mountain (Wenbishan) 9 kilometres (5.5 miles) south of Lijiang. The mountain, steep and pointed, is the most conspicuous within the Huangshan Range. The road to Wenfengsi passes through Baihua, the richest village in the entire region. At the foot of the mountain it begins a long climb along a rugged dirt track. It is much nicer to leave the car here and walk straight up to the temple through orchards and woods, silent save for the birds. This once-famous complex is now a ruin, looked after by two old monks, but it is still a marvellous and holy place, hidden within a glade surrounded by giant, shady trees. Amidst the destruction there remain some gems of painting and carving: Tibetan mandalas and writing, the Eight Sacred Emblems of Buddhism, roof murals (still bright and beautiful) and six central square red columns with lotiform capitals.

Wenfengsi was a centre for occult and ascetic practices. Just above the temple at the edge of the forest is a sacred spring where initiates underwent an amazing training. A simple hole in the earth nearby became the home of an ascetic who would proceed to spend three years, three months, three days and three hours within, meditating, reciting sutras, praying and doing battle with psychic demons. Local monks would think nothing of striking out on foot for a two- or three-year walk to the great pilgrimage sites of Tibet. If you want a good hike, it is a three-hour walk from the temple ruins to the top of holy Wenbishan.

Zhiyunsi, the fourth main temple, has been converted into a school for the children of Lashiba, a town southwest of Lijiang.

Nothing remains of **Kingdom of Blessing Temple** (Fuguosi), oldest of the five temples, except for one small house. Two important buildings were transported intact from the original site to Black Dragon Pool Park in Lijiang in recent years.

Dragon Spring Temple (Longquansi)

This minor temple lies west of Lijiang near the village of Wenmingcun at the base of low pine-covered hills. Longquansi is thoroughly dilapidated but has a kind of random beauty about it. A compact and cosy courtyard is filled with primula, orchids, peach trees, citrus and roses. The god at the main table altar is in the *dongba* style and the nearby Chinese characters mean 'happiness for every family'. The murals are all ruined but some excellent wood carving remains on doors, windows and railings, with motifs from Daoism, Buddhism and animism.

Baisha Village and Great Precious Storehouse Temple (Dabaoji Gong)

Baisha is the most important village on the plain north of Lijiang. It was the Naxi capital before Kublai Khan came south to claim this region as part of the Yuan Empire (1279–1368), at which time Lijiang was made the centre. The name Baisha is the sinicized form of Boashi, which means 'dead Pumi', a reference to the victorious battle and slaughter of the Pumi tribe in ancient times.

Great Precious Storehouse Temple is also known as Coloured Glaze Temple (Liulidian). It can be found near the village school, which is itself a converted temple. The complex was built and decorated over a period of more than 200 years, from 1385 to 1619, employing the eclectic artistic energies of Chinese Daoists, Tibetan and Naxi Buddhists and local *dongba* shamans. This rich fusion has resulted in a tremendously powerful art, heavy in spirit and awe-inspiring in its presentation of the mystical world. Dominated by black, silver, dark green, gold and red colours, the murals in the back hall, overlaid with centuries of brown soot, are doom-laden and bizarre. The scenes and figures, some still vivid in detail, are largely taken from Tibetan Lamaist iconography and include the Wheel of Life, judges of the underworld, the damned, titans and gods, Buddhas and bodhisattvas. There are trigrams, lotus flowers and even Sanskrit inscriptions on the ceiling. The deliberate damage done to the paintings is apparent and terrible, but the loss of the irreplaceable wooden statuary that filled the temple, of which there is no trace, is even more tragic.

A separate building called **Pavilion of Great Calm** (Dadingge) stands outside the front wall of the main temple. Although built later, in the Qing Dynasty (1644–1911), it is considered part of the whole grouping, and though badly damaged has some exquisite, delicate paintings of flowers, birds and jewellery.

Great Precious Storehouse Temple is officially open from 9 am to 4 pm every day but this is fanciful. If the gate is locked ask around until you find Mr He Zhengong. He holds the key.

Jade Dragon Snow Range (Yulongxueshan)

The formidable Jade Dragon Mountains dominate the Lijiang Plain, defining its western edge with their towering mass. The mountains' western flanks drop steeply to the Upper Yangzi River (Jinsha Jiang), helping to form deep, awe-inspiring gorges.

Unlikely as it may seem in this age of competition and nonpareil mountaineers, no human has yet conquered the Jade Dragon. Largely because of bad weather, Japanese, American and People's Liberation Army expeditions have all failed in their bids to scale Shanzidou, at 5,596 metres

(18,360 feet) the highest peak. Storms frequently rage around the glaciers, rocks and perpetual snowfields of the five primary summits. However, the alpine meadows on the lower slopes, where herders sing to their goats and cattle and collectors of wild medicinal herbs go happily about their business, are excellent hiking country. Such excursions are a natural extension of visits to the many temple sites around Lijiang.

Stone Drum (Shigu)

The village of Stone Drum stands at the First Great Bend of the Yangzi River, 70 kilometres (44 miles) west of Lijiang. The route from Lijiang follows the main road to Dali for 45 kilometres (28 miles), then branches west by a good, unpaved road that winds downward towards the river through huge forests.

The approach to Stone Drum offers a dramatic view of the Yangzi's near-180-degree turn, where the wide, swift waters perform a miraculous about-face. For nearly 20 kilometres (12.5 miles) the river, first flowing south, then north, runs parallel to itself. Locals say if it were not for their village standing guard at the bend, China would lose the water of the Yangzi to Southeast Asia, like that of the adjacent Mekong and Salween Rivers.

Stone Drum gets its name from a large, cylindrical, marble tablet shaped like a drum, an engraved memorial that honours the Sino-Naxi victory over a Tibetan army in the summer of 1548. It was an awful slaughter on the banks of the river. A Tibetan force of 200,000 men was completely routed and dispersed in confusion, and in gory celebration the champions decapitated nearly 3,000 of the enemy. The stone drum recounts it all: '. . . heads heaped like grave mounds, blood like rain. . .'.

Another military event occurred here in recent times, a small but important chapter in the story of the Long March, Chinese communism's greatest ordeal. After breaking out of the Nationalist encirclement in eastern China at the end of 1934, the Red Army of 100,000 fled westward, embarking on an epic 6,000-kilometre (3,750-mile) march through some of the country's most bitter, rugged land before finding a haven in Shaanxi Province. The main body of the army crossed the Yangzi several hundred kilometres east of Stone Drum, but 18,000 men crossed at this point. The citizenry rose to the occasion, ceaselessly ferrying troops to the northern bank in their boats, 40−60 men per trip. The entire crossing took four days and nights (24−28 April 1936) and is still remembered as the greatest event in the lives of the local Naxi. The prominent marble 'Chinese Workers and Peasants Red Army Second Route Army Long March Ferry Crossing Memorial' stands on a high promontory with a fine view over the historic site.

Tiger Leaping Gorge (Hutiaoxia)

After the renowned Three Gorges (Sanxia) in Sichuan and Hubei, Hutiao-xia is the Yangzi's best known gorge. Wedged tightly between titanic cliffs, the river is so narrow here, so legend tells us, that a hunted tiger made his escape to the other side in a single bound. Yunnan's main northern road to Tibet crosses the Yangzi near the gorge at Lunan, 90 kilometres (56 miles) from Lijiang. From the road it is possible to see how such a geological phenomenon was created: two huge mountains leaning close to each other and a large volume of fast moving water between them cutting deeper and deeper into the bottom of the gorge. In some places there is a sheer drop of 3,000 metres (10,000 feet) to the water, an altogether beautiful and vertiginous place to go for a walk.

Dry Sea (Ganhai)

The Dry Sea is a section of the Lijiang Plain 22 kilometres (14 miles) north of the city that receives less rain than other areas. The road runs straight through the middle of the valley, parallel to the mountains on the left. Agriculture is replaced by the rock-strewn plain of Amendu, a curious name meaning 'Rocks Without Tails'. The road rises slowly but steadily until it crosses a gentle pass and breaks up into random tracks that criss-cross one another in a dry 'sea' of short brown grass, sand and stones. Occasional lone pines break the monotony as the road skirts the base of the mountains, giving an exceptional close view of the Jade Dragon massif.

Black Water, White Water (Heibaishui)

The road picks up again at the far edge of the Dry Sea and climbs into the mountains past vistas of long, forested valleys with no sign of human habitation. Water is finally reached after several kilometres at the swift river of White Water (Baishui), named for the white stones in the riverbed. The limestone, washed down from mountain peaks, sometimes contains recognizable coral, proof that this land once lay deep below the ocean. Further up the mountain rushes Black Water (Heishui) in a bed of black rock. Tradition dictates that you drink only the white water.

Roads and logging camps in the area have changed traditional patterns of tribal interaction and now Naxi meet and mingle with the indigenous Yi, who, with 30 branches and distribution over four provinces, are China's fourth largest minority.

Nguluko, the home of Joseph Rock

Nguluko (Chinese: Xuesongcun, Snow Pine Village) is a small, typical Naxi village, whose lovely name in the local language means 'at the foot of the silver stone mountain'. It lies slightly north of Jade Lake Village (Yuhucun) and is unremarkable except for being touched by a remarkable man.

In 1922 an Austro-American botanist and explorer named Joseph Rock arrived in Lijiang and made this area his home on and off for the next 29 years. He was a contrary man of tremendous energy and terrible temper who lived like a foreign prince in the wilds of western China, always engaged in activities from plant collecting and surveying to photography and linguistics. His prodigious output of articles and books and contributions to several sciences is impressive. He will probably be best remembered for the introduction of innumerable plant species to the West and his rigorous works on Naxi ethnology.

Nguluko, Rock's country home, was where he kept his retinue of a dozen Naxi servants perpetually busy, pressing plants for herbaria, summing up the discoveries and specimens of the last expedition or preparing for the next one. His house still stands, and is today owned by one of the last remainders of a bygone era, Li Wenbiao, Rock's own muleteer. Mr Li does not speak much Chinese but he will welcome you with a generous heart into a courtyard that once witnessed the energy and accomplishments of a strange and splendid man. The house is a good example of Naxi domestic architecture; a wall and gateway that open onto a three-sided courtyard, the residence ahead, and the wood and animal shelters aside.

Inscribed Stone at Jade Lake Village (Yuhucun)

A historically important monument stands at the back of Jade Lake Village near the base of the mountains, 15 kilometres (9.5 miles) northwest of Lijiang. It is an 18-metre (59-foot) high limestone wall inscribed with the two epigraphs 'a jade pillar supports Heaven' and 'jade wall and golden river', the latter a reference to the Jade Dragon Mountains and the Golden Sands River (Jinsha Jiang, common name for the Upper Yangzi). A Qing-Dynasty official, representative of the emperor, completed the inscription in 1724, thus imprinting the fateful year that marked full Chinese control over Naxi political life.

Beyond Heibaishui

Downstream from the confluence of Heibaishui lies the small community of **Jiazi**, and further still downstream the fascinating town of **Dadong**, a traditional Naxi community. Twenty kilometres (13 miles) to the northeast of Dadong on the Yangzi lies **Hongmenkou**, the site where Kublai Khan's army made the treacherous river crossing on inflated skin boats in the 13th century. Farther north still is the ancient walled town of **Baoshan**, one of the last of its kind in China.

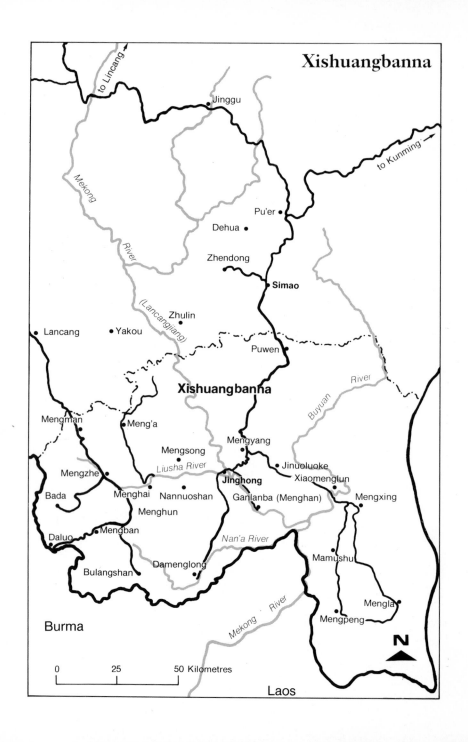

Xishuangbanna

Yunnan's southernmost region, bordering Burma and Laos, is officially known as the Xishuangbanna Dai Autonomous Prefecture. The Dai are one of Yunnan's major minority groups, numbering nearly 800,000 throughout the province, and nearly a third of these reside in Xishuangbanna.

This long and evocative name is actually a sinicized form of the Dai *sip song bana* which simply means 'twelve administrative units', a nomenclature from the late 16th century.

Xishuangbanna lies just below the Tropic of Cancer. It is a marvellously rich and fecund area, holding fully one-quarter of China's faunal species and one-sixth of its plant species. There are only two seasons here, hot and dry, and hot and wet. Monsoon rains usually arrive in June, are heaviest in August and September, and finally let up in October.

In the past, rain, humidity, heat and isolation, combined with actual diseases, earned Xishuangbanna the grim sobriquet 'land of lethal vapours'. Any man planning a trip there was strongly advised to say a final goodbye to his wife and get a coffin ready. Malaria and cholera were perennial killers, and in 1929 bubonic plague wiped out a large section of the population. Since the 1950s steady progress has been made in public health and it is now perfectly safe to travel in Xishuangbanna.

The early history of the Dai is lost to an ancient, pre-literate age, but there are clearly linguistic and cultural links between these graceful, slim-waisted people and those in Thailand. The questions of common ancestry and migration have not been conclusively answered, however, and many theories, some self-serving, continue to contradict one another.

A lyrical origination story stands firmly in the hearts of the people. In the beginning Xishuangbanna was a vast ocean which in time subsided to reveal a lush and bountiful paradise. The Dai flourished and wanted for nothing until jealous demons waged bloody war and seized the land. Awful slaughter and misery descended, birds and insects ceased their music-making and even the light of day disappeared. The land was plunged into total darkness.

This impossible situation was challenged by a brave and resolute young man who led his people in a life-and-death struggle against the demons. The enemy was forced to retreat and the demon-king leapt into the Mekong River to escape. The tireless youth pursued and they fought a seven-day battle beneath the rushing water. Victory came at last and the Dai hero emerged with a magical pearl taken from the demon's throat. He hung this high in a tree where its radiance lit up the land, and to this very day the capital of Xishuangbanna is called Jinghong, the City of Dawn, in remembrance of that mythical day.

The first actual records appear in the second century BC, when the Han Dynasty acknowledged tributary missions from Dai chieftains. From the eighth to 12th centuries Xishuangbanna was incorporated into the Nanzhao and Dali Kingdoms, and only after that time did it become a vassal of China, one of the empire's most god-forsaken outposts. In 1570 a Ming Bureau of Pacification was established to intensify control over border areas; this style of administration continued well into the Qing Dynasty, but as the Manchu world became increasingly moribund in the late 19th century, colonial powers stepped in. First France, with its neighbouring Indo-Chinese territories, toyed with encroachment and then Britain actually occupied Jinghong with a force of 500 troops. In the end, however, both powers decided to keep Xishuangbanna as a buffer zone.

During the first half of the 20th century Xishuangbanna was controlled by a Chinese warlord and by an ancient, stifling system imposed by indigenous overlords. For the common people 'the water they drank, the road they walked on, the quarters they dwelled in, the very earth which covered their faces at death' were all subject to taxation.

The People's Liberation Army entered Xishuangbanna in 1950 but was not greeted as heir to the Legend of the Pearl. Rather, the Dai mistrusted the Chinese soldiers and saw them as a new wave of oppressors. In time confidence grew between both groups and, despite cruelties during the Cultural Revolution, Han-Dai relations are good and Xishuangbanna is one of the most successfully integrated minority areas in China.

Getting to Xishuangbanna

The commonest way to reach Xishuangbanna is by flying to the regional centre of Simao and then carrying on by bus or taxi to Jinghong, Xishuangbanna's capital. Vintage Soviet prop planes leave from Kunming every day except Wednesday and Sunday for the 75-minute flight to Simao.

Strong winds above the mountains of central Yunnan frequently cause flight delays so it is common to spend a night in Simao, either going to, or returning from, Xishuangbanna. The **Simao District Guesthouse** (Simao Diqu Zhaodaisuo) is where foreigners stay; it has adequate double rooms (Rmb40 per day) with private bathrooms and a good dining room. Local specialities include fried wasp larva, steamed frog, monkey and a strong, sweet, piquant corn brew.

It is important to remember to bring enough money with you from Kunming for the entire trip to Xishuangbanna.

There are two main ways to pass a few hours in Simao. One is to visit the **Plum River Reservoir Park** (Meizihe Shuiku Gongyuan), 7 kilometres (4.5 miles) southeast of the town. Here there are paddle boats, clean water and quiet surroundings — a good place to swim or relax. The

second way is to explore Simao on foot and discover the old wooden town, secreted away behind the broad, dusty main thoroughfares. The old houses and cobbled alleys crowd together on a hill east of the main north-south road. There you can see little teashops, beautifully carved lintels and window frames, stacks of firewood, pack animals — in short, a way of life that is rapidly being usurped by modernization and new construction.

The 165-kilometre (103-mile) overland trip from Simao to Jinghong takes four to five hours along a paved, mountain road. At the 33-kilometre (20-mile) marker there is a checkpoint for all vehicles passing from Simao District into Xishuangbanna's Jinghong County. After this the road rambles on, occasionally traversing narrow plains of rice and sugar cane, with tea and rubber growing on hillsides near the villages. But parts of the trip cut through Rousseau-like jungles, lush and fecund, filled with impenetrable greenery. The road finally comes out high above a river valley and then rapidly descends towards the huge yellow bends of the silt-filled Mekong River. Jinghong, the destination, lies on its west bank.

An alternative way to reach Jinghong from Kunming is to make the entire trip by bus, a 740-kilometre (462-mile) adventure. This takes up to three-and-a-half days and requires spending nights in small hostelries along the way; the common stops are at Eshan, Yuanjiang or Mojiang. Tickets for this long-distance bus can be bought at the main Passenger Transport Bus Station near the railway station.

Hotels in Xishuangbanna

Number One Guesthouse
(Diyi Zhaodaisuo)
Galan Lu, Jinghong

第一招待所
嘎兰路

Standard double Rmb40, dormitory Rmb4

Nearly every visitor to Xishuangbanna stays at this guesthouse. The original compound, built in 1955 and surrounded by flowering bougain-villaea, retains the quality of a faded resort villa. The best rooms are still in the old buildings. New structures have been added so that the complex can now handle up to 300 people. Most guests eat at the guesthouse's good though somewhat pricey restaurant.

Tropical Crops Research Institute Guesthouse

热带作物研究所
招待所

24 rooms and a large dining room; Rmb12 per person

This small guesthouse, located on the Institute grounds near the pond, welcomes foreign guests. This is the only alternative to staying at the Number One Guesthouse.

Food and Drink in Xishuangbanna

Xishuangbanna's tropical climate allows for a rich variety of delicious, exotic food. Fruit lovers will be happy here with a changing seasonal collection of bananas, papayas, mangoes, pineapples, lychees, jackfruits, breadfruits and many others.

The Dai pay special attention to their rice, its texture, size, colour, taste and 'perfume'. Two special varieties are glutinous rice (*nuomi*), generally cooked in a mould with meat, fish, egg or sweet filling, similar to Chinese rice dumplings (*zhongzi*), and *zimi*, a purple-hued rice much prized for its colour and flavour, steamed inside a cylindrical section of bamboo.

If you are lucky enough to be invited into a Dai house for a banquet, or want to arrange a visit through CITS (approximately Rmb30 per person), a typical menu might include the following dishes:

Zucchini with special fragrant herbs
Mild pickled bamboo shoots
Minced meat steamed in banana leaves
Fish in a thick sauce with garlic sprouts
Spicy chicken
Biandou, *a large flat bean served with tomato purée*
Qingta, *crisp fried sheets of water vegetable*
Pea-shoot soup
Sesame beef
Fried banana
Sweets and green tea

All of the above are accompanied by overflowing bowls of strong, white liquor. Such an evening, sitting in low bamboo chairs, surrounded by friendly people, listening to the soft night noises, is an unforgettable experience.

Sights in Xishuangbanna

Jinghong

The small, sleepy capital of Xishuangbanna, despite its broad avenues and Chinese-style cement buildings, has all the feelings of an upland Southeast Asian town. There is an unhurried ease here that has charm if your expectations are in tempo with the place. As the head of the local Foreign Affairs Bureau says, 'There is really not much going on here.'

He is not entirely correct. Foreign visitors invariably leave Xishuang-banna with a quizzical sense of having been to a special place, far from the crush of China proper, a land filled with kind, gentle people.

Jinghong comes alive on market and festival days, but for the most part

its commercial life is lmited to the handful of shops along the main street, with their weird assortment of goods, and to the rows of outdoor vendors in the northern part of town — watch and bicycle repairmen, clothing stalls, hat sellers and fruiterers. Minority clothing and crafts are available in the markets.

Jinghong is a good place for strolling, whether it be down to the banks of the Mekong River or southward to the traditional Dai stilt-housed villages that make up the suburbs. Jinghong is the base and starting point for all excursions into the hinterlands of Xishuangbanna.

Tropical Crops Research Institute

In the western suburbs of Jinghong lies the Tropical Crops Research Institute, a large, well laid out estate with a beautiful palm-lined entranceway. Its staff of 1,300 looks after the grounds and conducts research in a number of fields related to economic plants. The institute manages a vast rubber plantation that contributes significantly to its annual revenue of nearly US$15 million. Tapping of the rubber trees begins at the end of March and continues uninterrupted for nine months, at which time the trees need to rest.

In the midst of the rubber forest is a large cement memorial. Every visitor to the institute will be told the story of how, on 14 April 1961, Premier Zhou Enlai met with Premier U Nu at this spot to discuss the Sino-Burmese border situation.

Within sight of the main building are long gardens containing dozens of plant species with economic and medicinal importance to man. Pepper, oil palm, cinnamon, cocoa pods, nutmeg, sesame are here in abundance.

The Water Splashing Festival (Poshui Jie)

The Dai Lunar New Year, commonly called the Water Splashing Festival, is marked each April by three days of unbridled celebration, drunkenness and hilarity. It is a wonderful time to be in Xishuangbanna, but because of transportation and lodging constraints only about 300 foreigners, many of them students studying in China, are able to attend.

The festival is similar to Thailand's Songkran celebration and has its origin rooted in the theme of titanic struggle between the forces of good and evil. As the story goes, the Dai people were subjugated by demons who possessed magical forces. The demon-king had seven beautiful consorts, the last of whom was a kind-hearted lady who wanted to help her people. One evening, by plying the wicked king with drink and feigning loving concern, she extracted the secret of his vulnerability. His neck was tender and weak — he could be strangled easily. When the demon-king dozed off, the brave maiden plucked a single white hair from his head, wrapped it around his neck and pulled with all her might. Not only did the king die, but his head came off entirely and to everyone's dismay erupted into a violent fountain of froth, blood and fire. Flames threatened to engulf the entire land so in desperation each of the seven women took turns holding the head while the others poured water on it to wash away the blood and quell the flames. The spell was finally broken, peace and tranquillity returned to the land and ever since the people have celebrated the Water Splashing Festival, to honour their release and to wash away the sins, ignorance and obstacles of the previous year.

Today, despite opposition from many local Dai, the government has standardized the date of the festival rather then letting it range over weeks as it did in the past. It is fixed for 13 −18 April, with three main days of activities. These include fiercely competitive dragon-boat races on the river, parades, giant sky-rockets, songs in the streets, buffalo slaughter, with much eating and drinking and splashing water everywhere. It is impossible to stay dry; be careful of your camera.

The outstanding feature of the Water Splashing Festival is the gathering of so many different minority groups in one place, all dressed in their finest clothing, for several joyous days of singing, dancing and revelry.

Menghai

Travelling from Jinghong through the valley of the Flowing Sands River (Liushahe) brings one to Menghai, one of the rare broad plains of Xishuangbanna, a region of 'bounty and delight' for the Dai people. Menghai's relatively high altitude of 1,400 metres (4,600 feet) limits it to one rice crop per year but the weather is perfect for tea. In fact this is one of the great tea regions of China, providing Hong Kong with most of its beloved *pu'er* tea, Tibet with essential tea bricks, and France with a popular and profitable tea for slimming, *tuocha*. The Menghai Tea Factory (Menghai Chachang) is the largest industrial employer in Xishuangbanna. Arrangements to visit the tea factory can be made through CITS.

Menghai lies 53 kilometres (33 miles) west of Jinghong and has a government guesthouse (*zhaodaisuo*) for simple accommodation 1 kilometre (0.6 mile) south of the main market road.

Octagonal Pagoda (Bajiaoting)

Under a guise of different names, the Octagonal Pagoda is the most famous architectural site in Xishuangbanna. It stands on a man-made hill 15 kilometres (8 miles) west of Menghai, just off the main road, near Jingzhen Village; it is also known as Jingzhen Pagoda (Jingzhenta).

The story of the temple's construction revolves around two pious locals who wanted to honour the Buddha and put an end to a tyranny of marauding wasps, at the same time. Between the years 1698−1701 they super-

vised the construction of a wasp-displacing hill, built the temple and encouraged religious gatherings. Their masterpiece, renovated four times, is now a protected cultural monument. The temple has an overall feeling of compactness, intricacy and richness. Its heavy coloured base of alternating hues — blue, yellow, green, red and glass-covered stripes, anchors the brick bottom to the earth. Higher up on a deep, reddish-brown background, gold designs of flowers, stupas, trees, *dharma* wheels, *chakras* and geometric forms create an interim level. Finally, the fantastic eight-sectioned, ten-tiered roof rises steeply to a round, scaloped cupola, topped by a Buddha-spire of hoops and dangling metal objects. Careful scruitny will reveal many details and mythical beasts on the 16-metre (53-foot) high pagoda.

Three surrounding buildings on the hilltop, built in 1985, now house a library and living quarters for the local monks.

Mengzhe

Nearly 20 kilometres (19 miles) beyond Menghai lies the town of Mengzhe,in the heart of tea growing country. There are several pagodas in the area; the best known is Manlei Great Buddha Pagoda, with two large painted stupas. The central one rises 20 metres (66 feet) high from a square base. The main body of the stupa is a heavy, tapering cylinder, topper with a spire and intricate filigree.

Banla Hani Village

After the Dai, the Hani People are the most common minority group in Xishuangbanna. A stop at Banla is the easiest way to see a mountain village in its naturalness and material simplicity. Although perhaps overburdened by foreigners because of its closeness to the main Jinghong-Menghai road, the Hani (Aini) here will not flaunt their 'ethnicity'. Visitors are advised to be circumspect and polite after crossing the Flowing Sands River into Hani territory. A path leads upward past the houses into mountains beyond, affording a beautiful view in several directions if you climb high enough.

Banla lies 37 kilometres (23 miles) west of Jinghong.

King of Tea Trees at Nannuoshan

A rutted, dirt jeep track leads south from the main road, 35 kilometres (21 miles) west of Jinghong. It climbs steadily up Nannuoshan for 8 kilometres (5 miles) to a small, flat clearing, the point of departure for a long, 817-step descent by foot to the King of Tea Trees. This 800-year old botanical wonder is reputed to have been planted by ancestors of the local Aini (Hani) minority. It stands 5.5 metres (18 feet) and helps support the theory that all tea in the world originated in southern Yunnan Province.

In most areas of China, rice grows submerged in water but some varieties, known as upland rice, grow in the earth with little or no irrigation. Nannuoshan gets its name, Southern Glutinous Rice Mountain, from the type of rice that is cultivated on its slopes by the Aini people. Farther up the mountain live the Lahu in clustered villages.

The Mekong River (Lancangjiang) and Olive Plain (Ganlanba)

The mighty Mekong, third longest river in China and 13th longest in the world, surges through the middle of Xishuangbanna, past Jinghong and onward to Laos. It is spanned at only a few points; one of these is the vital Jinghong Bridge, built in 1960 to link the entire region by road with Kunming.

The Mekong is navigable for nearly 320 kilometres (200 miles) inside Yunnan, but for visitors there is one main river trip southward to the state-run agricultural farm of the Olive Plain (Ganlanba). A boat leaves every morning at 8 am from under the big bridge for the one-hour trip downstream. Early morning mists frequently obscure the scenery but, in the afternoon, the longer return voyage upstream is almost always clear.

There is no boat at all during the dry spring months when the river is low. Public buses leave each morning from Jinghong's main bus station and travel down the east bank of the Mekong to the Olive Plain.

Large plantations of rubber and fruit trees cover the expansive Olive Plain. They are interspersed with brilliant emerald rice fields, random groves of coconut palms and occasional tea fields. The local Dai people call the area Menghan, which is also the name of the main town. Here daily markets attract a variety of minority groups from the surrounding country-side. Han Chinese, though certainly evident, only began settling in southern Xishuangbanna in the late 1950s.

The serenity of the Olive Plain is best experienced by walking from village to village, under large trees and along shaded paths which lead past ample wooden houses on stilts. There is always a scene of peaceful activity by the river; women washing, children playing or fetching water, fishing boats returning home with their catch.

In the village of Manting the Weijiang Baita pagoda has been rebuilt. This historically important religious structure dates back to the 12th century and was considered one the finest Burmese-style pagodas in China. Tragedy struck during the 1960s when Red Guards used dynamite to blow it up. The present huge structure was completed in March 1985 but the craftsmanship in no way approaches its predecessor. Other pagodas are scattered about the Olive Plain.

There are two simple but adequate hotels in Menghan for tourists who want to stay for several days, and numerous small restaurants along the main market street.

Damenglong and the White and Black Pagodas (Baita, Heita)

Southwest of Jinghong, only 8 kilometres (5 miles) from Burma, lies the village of Damenglong and its well-known pagodas. The 70-kilometre (44-mile) trip takes two hours on dusty, unpaved roads though stops along the way can turn this outing into a full-day trip.

The first sight, just beyond the turn-off from the main highway, is **Manguanglong Monastery** where it is possible to see the life of a religious community, with 30 or so young Buddhist monks and their two caring, yet stern, teachers who look after the education and development of the boys. The entranceway is flanked by two long undulating 'dragons'. The dominant building is a temple hall for prayer and recitation from *lontar-palm* sutras. It houses a large, crude Buddha statue and many strips of white and coloured cloth offerings.

If you visit the monastery, there are certain rules of courtesy to follow: do not touch the heads of monks; do not expose the soles of your shoes or feet in the direction of a person; take your shoes off when entering a temple; always respect the image of the Buddha and use care and discretion when taking photographs.

Down the road is **Manfeilong Reservoir**, a good place for boating, swimming or picnicking. From here, the route winds across the countryside, through valleys of rice, up and over hills covered with neat rows of rubber trees, past sections of jungle and eventually to **Xiaogai**, centre of the Dong Feng State Farm and host to a large Sunday market.

Beyond Xiaogai, shortly before Damenglong, is Manfeilong on the right side of the road. Atop a hill behind this village stands White Pagoda, a 13th-century structure that has had innumerable restorations. It is now made largely of cement, supported on two great concentric circular bases. Eight small stupas surround a taller, central spire. Local people describe the configuration, especially after a rainfall, as a cluster of spring bamboo shoots breaking through the earth as a vegetarian offering to the Buddha.

At the eastern base of the pagoda there is a little red door. It stays locked most of the time but an old caretaker, if asked politely, will open the door to reveal a shrine overflowing with offerings of money, flowers, fruit and embroidered cloth. The object of devotion is a pair of oversized 'footprints of the Buddha', a religious constant throughout the Buddhist world, a little like splinters of the Original Cross to Christians.

The outside of the pagoda is painted in horizontal stripes of bright, primary colours with white designs, and is inlaid with chips of mirror. This gaudiness is offset by the overall grace and balance of the pagoda; for outrageous, humorous crudity, the side prayer hall has a bestiary of dragons, unicorns, lion-dogs and a comical elephant.

The White Pagoda is perhaps the finest example of a Burmese-style pagoda in Xishuangbanna, along with one in Mengla which is,

unfortunately, off limits to foreigners.

In the distance, across a small valley just south of Damenglong, can be seen another pagoda. This is the undistinguished Black Pagoda, in fact a dirty-white structure with one main stupa and four smaller ones on the corners of a square cement base. Clumsy workmanship is everywhere, but the tinkling bells and isolation, fine view and cool breezes afford some redemption for the effort of climbing to this spot.

The Jinuo

The Jinuo people are the most recent group in China to be recognized as a distinct minority nationality. Before this official status was granted them by the central government in Beijing in 1979, the Jinuo, though known as hill-dwellers who subsisted primarily by slash-and-burn agriculture, lived largely out of reach of state aid programs. Today their lot has improved considerably. They number around 12,000 and live in approximately 40 villages of the **Jinuoluoke Mountains**. Their homeland is also known as Youleshan, a Chinese transliteration from the Jinuo language, meaning 'place the Han (Chinese) cannot find'.

The main settlement of Jinuoluoke lies 20 kilometres (12.5 miles) southeast of Mengyang on the road to the Tropical Botanical Garden at Xiaomenglun (see below). Arrangements to visit the Jinuo should be made through CITS.

Tropical Botanical Garden at Xiaomenglun

Thrusting deep into a bend of the Luosuo River is a narrow peninsula fancifully named Calabash Island (Huludao). There is nothing fanciful, however, about its 3,000 species of plants, one of the richest botanical concentrations in the world.

This is the home of Xishuangbanna's Tropical Botanical Garden, an institution founded in 1958 by dedicated scientists who simply set up shop in the jungle. Today there are nearly 500 workers who conduct important research in the areas of medicinal plants, taxonomy, economic plants and biochemistry.

For visitors who are not specialists, visiting here is like stepping into a bizarre and enchanted garden. A canopy of giant palms blocks out the sun, thick lily-pads act as boats for children, camphor trees fill the air with pungency, large bamboos reach heavenward. There is edification as well as pleasure; many plant species at the Botanical Garden carry nameplates to explain their usefulness to man and nature.

Xiaomenglong lies 103 kilometres (65 miles) southeast of Jinghong.

(preceding page) Banla Hani Village, at the foot of Nannuoshan
Mosu Naxi woman, Ninglang, northeast of Lijiang

Other Places in Yunnan Province

A province as large and varied as Yunnan cannot be fully embraced or savoured in one or even several trips. The main entries in this book — Kunming, the Stone Forest, Dali, Lijiang and Xishuangbanna — are clearly the best places to start, but now other little known towns and areas are opening to foreign visitors. Below are some alternative destinations.

Qujing, on the main railway line to Guizhou Province, is a town of 50,000 people in the pretty red and green mountains of eastern Yunnan. It was an important transport centre for the Allied Forces during World War II.

Southeast of Kunming, beyond Lake Dianchi, lies the province's deepest body of water, crystal clear **Fuxian Lake**. Traditional fishing villages dot the shore, and along the eastern edge of the lake fishermen still practise an ancient fishing technique. 'Fish ditches' (*yugou*), stone-lined channels that lead from the cold lake to warmer entrapment pools, prove irresistible to large, succulent fish, where they can be gathered up with no effort at all.

Farther south still, lies **Jiangchuan**, a wealthy county seat 100 kilometres (63 miles) from Kunming. It has a good county guesthouse (*xian zhaodaisuo*), good food and friendly people. The important Bronze-Age site of Lijiashan, excavated in 1972, is near Jiangchuan.

East of Jiangchuan, in a fertile and well-populated valley, stands **Yuxi**, the modern district capital. It is an important secondary city with diversified industries. Although not yet geared for tourists it is worth a visit to see the cigarette factory and the mix of urban and rural prosperity.

The town of **Tonghai** was devastated by an earthquake in 1970 but has re-established itself as an important market centre. It lies in picturesque countryside on the south side of Tonghai Lake, a pleasant area for walking and exploring. Approximately 8 kilometres (5 miles) west of the town is Xinmeng, a remarkable community of three clustered villages. The residents are Mongolians, the last remaining descendants of Kublai Khan's conquering army of the 13th century.

Although only open to foreigners with special permission, two outstanding places in the westernmost part of Yunnan are worth mentioning.

Baoshan is a large district capital located on a broad plain 600 kilometres (375 miles) by road from Kunming. This plain witnessed a titanic battle between the army of the King of Mian (Burma) and Kublai Khan's Mongolian warriors. The vastly superior Burmese forces, with armoured elephant, had the upper hand until brilliant tactics won the day for the Mongols.

Several minority groups live in and around Baoshan, notably the Hui (Muslims), Yi and Dai.

There is regular air service from Kunming to Baoshan five time a week.

Yunnan's westernmost spur of land, known as the Dehong region, reaches far into Burma and is the home of two minority groups, the Jingpo and Dai. These Dehong Dai are considered by many Chinese to be even more handsome and refined than their brethren in Xishuangbanna. Their town of **Ruili** is also seen as one of the most pleasing and exotic places in the entire province.

In the far northwest of Yunnan lies a prefecture inhabited almost entirely by Tibetans. The road from Lijiang to Tibet passes through **Zhongdian**, a large town on the edge of the Tibetan Plateau. Nearby Zhongdian lie the ruins of the once grand Jietang Songlinsi, a huge monastery of the Yellow Hat sect. It was destroyed but today Buddhism is returning and the faithful are rebuilding the monastic community. More than 300 monks in nearby villages have again taken up the ecclesiastical life.

A Guide to Pronouncing Chinese Names

The official system of romanization used in China, which the visitor will find on maps, road signs and city shopfronts, is known as *Pinyin*. It is now almost universally adopted by the western media.

Non-Chinese may initially encounter some difficulty in pronouncing romanized Chinese words. In fact many of the sounds correspond to the usual pronunciation of the letters in English. The exceptions are:

Initials

c	is like the *ts* in '*its*'
q	is like the *ch* in '*ch*eese'
x	has no English equivalent, and can best be described as a hissing consonant that lies somewhere between *sh* and *s*. The sound was rendered as hs under an earlier transcription system.
z	is like the *ds* in 'fa*ds*'
zh	is unaspirated, and sounds like the *j* in '*j*ug'

Finals

a	sounds like 'ah'
e	is pronounced as in 'h*er*'
i	is pronounced as in 'sk*i*' (written as *yi* when not preceded by an initial consonant). However, in *ci, chi, ri, shi, zi* and *zhi*, the sound represented by the *i* final is quite different and is similar to the *ir* in 's*ir*', but without much stressing of the *r* syllable.
o	sounds like the *aw* in 'l*aw*'
u	sounds like the *oo* in '*oo*ze'
ê	is pronounced as in 'g*e*t'
ü	is pronounced as the German *ü* (written as *yu* when not preceded by an initial consonant)

The last two finals are usually written simply as *e* and *u*.

Finals in Combination

When two or more finals are combined, such as in *hao, jiao* and *liu*, each letter retains its sound value as indicated in the list above, but note the following:

ai	is like the *ie* in 't*ie*'
ei	is like the *ay* in 'b*ay*'
ian	is like the *ien* in 'Vi*enn*a'
ie	similar to 'ear'
ou	is like the *o* in 'c*o*de'
uai	sounds like 'why'

uan is like the *uan* in 'ig*uan*a'
(except when preceded by *j*, *q*, *x* and *y*; in these cases a *u* following any of these four consonants is in fact *ü* and *uan* is similar to *uen*.)
ue is like the *ue* in 'd*ue*t'
ui sounds like 'way'

Examples

A few Chinese names are shown below with English phonetic spelling beside them:

Beijing	Bay-jing
Cixi	Tsi-shi
Guilin	Gway-lin
Hangzhou	Hahng-jo
Kangxi	Kahn-shi
Qianlong	Chien-lawng
Tiantai	Tien-tie
Xi'an	Shi-ahn

An apostrophe is used to separate syllables in certain compound-character words to preclude confusion. For example, *Changan* (which can be *chang-an* or *chan-gan*) is sometimes written as *Chang'an*.

Tones

A Chinese syllable consists of not only an initial and a final or finals, but also a tone or pitch of the voice when the words are spoken. In *Pinyin* the four basic tones are marked ‾, ´, ˇ and `. These marks are almost never shown in printed form except in language texts.

Recommended Reading

General Background

Fairbank, John King. *The United States and China* (Cambridge: Harvard University Press, 1961)
Fairbank, John King et al. *East Asia: Tradition and Transformation* (London: George Allen & Unwin, 1973)
Polo, Marco; trans. R. E. Lathan. *The Travels of Marco Polo* (London: Penguin Books, 1958)
Spence, Jonathan. *The Gate of Heavenly Peace: The Chinese and their Revolution* (London: Faber and Faber, 1982)
Tuchman, Barbara. *Stilwell and the American Experience in China, 1911–45* (New York: The Macmillan Company, 1970)
Ward, Frank Kingdon. *Plant Hunting on the Edge of the World* (London: Cadogan Books, 1986)

Yunnan

Backus, Charles. *The Nan-chao Kingdom and Tang China's Southwestern Frontier* (Cambridge: Cambridge University Press, 1981)
Davies, Major H.R. *Yun-nan — The Link Between India and the Yangtze* (London: Cambridge University Press, 1909)
Fei, Hsiao-tung. *Earthbound China* (London: Routledge & Kegan Paul Ltd., 1949)
Fitzgerald, C.P. *The Tower of Five Glories: A Study of the Min Chia of Ta Li* (Connecticut: Hyperion Press Inc., 1973)
Fitzgerald, C.P. *The Yunnan-Burma Road* (London: Geographical Journal, Vol.95, 1940)
Goullart, Peter. *Forgotten Kingdom* (London: John Murray, 1957)
Hsu, Francis K. *Under the Ancestors's Shadow* (Stanford: Stanford University Press, 1975)
Rock, Joseph F. *The Ancient Na-Khi Kingdom of Southwest China* (Cambridge: Harvard University Press, 1947)
Rock, Joseph F. *Through the Great River Trenches of Asia* (Washington, D.C.: National Geographic Society, 1926)
Sutton, S.B. *In China's Border Provinces: The Turbulent Career of Joseph Rock, Botanist/Explorer* (New York: Hastings House, 1974)
Zhong, Xiu. *Yunnan Travelogue: 100 Days in Southwest China* (Beijing: New World Press, 1983)

(preceding page) Near the rugged eastern shore of Erhai Lake

Chronology of Periods in Chinese History

Palaeolithic	c.600,000−7000 BC
Neolithic	c.7000−1600 BC
Shang	c.1600−1027 BC
Western Zhou	1027−771 BC
Eastern Zhou	770−256 BC
Spring and Autumn Annals	770−476 BC
Warring States	475−221 BC
Qin	221−207 BC
Western (Former) Han	206 BC−8 AD
Xin	9−24
Eastern (Later) Han	25−220
Three Kingdoms	220−265
Western Jin	265−316
Northern and Southern Dynasties	317−589
Sixteen Kingdoms	317−439
□ Former Zhao	304−329
□ Former Qin	351−383
□ Later Qin	384−417
Northern Wei	386−534
Western Wei	535−556
Northern Zhou	557−581
Sui	581−618
Tang	618−907
Five Dynasties	907−960
Northern Song	960−1127
Southern Song	1127−1279
Jin (Jurchen)	1115−1234
Yuan (Mongol)	1279−1368
Ming	1368−1644
Qing (Manchu)	1644−1911
Republic	1911−1949
People's Republic	1949−

Useful Addresses in Kunming

Airline Office

Civil Aviation Administration of China (CAAC)
146 Dongfeng Dong Lu
Reservations tel. 24270
Cargo tel. 24650
中国民用航空　东风东路146号

Banks

Bank of China (Kunming Branch)
270–271 Huguo Lu
tel. 29601, tx. 64034
中国银行昆明分行　护国路270-271号

People's Bank of China (Yunnan Branch)
Zhengyi Lu
tel. 26972
中国人民银行云南分行　正义路

Cinemas and Theatres

Hongxing Theatre
Dongfeng Xi Lu
tel. 25275
红星剧院　东风西路

Kunming Theatre
Qingnian Lu
tel. 23722
昆明剧院　青年路

Panlong Theatre
202 Baoshan Jie
盘龙剧院　宝善街202号

Xinghuo Theatre
Baoshan Jie
tel. 24872
星火剧院　宝善街

Hospitals

Kunming Number One Affiliated Hospital
Zongshuying
tel. 25383
昆明医学院第一附属医院　棕树营

Yunnan Number One People's Hospital
173 Jinbi Lu
tel. 23480, 24238
云南第一人民医院　金碧路173号

Museum

Yunnan Provincial Museum
2 Wuyi Lu
tel. 23694, 24408
云南省博物馆　五一路2号

Post and Telecommunications

Customs and Post Office
555 Beijing Lu
tel. 24437, 27650
昆明海关及邮局　北京路555号

Main Post Office (Youdian Dalou)
Dongfeng Dong Lu at Beijing Lu
tel. 27319
昆明邮电大楼　东风东路

Public Security Bureau

Public Security Bureau (Gonganju)
Foreign Affairs Section
525 Beijing Lu
tel. 26191
(open 8–12 am, 2–6 pm)
昆明市公安局外事科　北京路525号

Shops

Antiques, Arts and Crafts

Friendship Store (top floor of Kunming Department Store)
99 Dongfeng Xi Lu
tel. 24698, 27188
友谊商店　东风西路99号

Yunnan Arts and Crafts Shop
529–530 Dongfeng Xi Lu
tel. 26871
云南省工艺美术服务部
东风西路529-530号

Yunnan Antiques and Curios Store
Kewen Dalou, Nantaiqiao
云南省文物商店分店　南太桥科文大楼

Department Stores

Kunming Department Store (Number One Department Store)
99 Dongfeng Xi Lu
昆明百货大楼　东风西路99号

Dongfeng Department Store (Number Two Department Store)
59 Dongfeng Xi Lu
东风百货商店　东风西路59号

Minorities Department Store
46–49 Nanping Jie
tel. 25171
(special shop for tourists upstairs)
民族贸易商店　南屏街46-49号

Books

Foreign Languages Bookstore
Kewen Dalou, Nantaiqiao
tel. 26261
外文书店　南太桥科文大楼

Xinhua Bookstore (Children's books, posters, maps)
107–108 Dongfeng Dong Lu
tel. 24490
新华书店　东风东路107-108号

Xinhua Bookstore (General books)
17 Dongfeng Xi Lu
新华书店　东风西路17号

Miscellaneous

Zhengyi Photographic Shop
109 Zhengyi Lu
tel. 26405
正义照拍器材商店　昆明市正义路109号

Travel and Transport

Kunming Airport
Wujiaba
tel. 22234
(7.5 kilometres/4.6 miles from town)
昆明机场　巫家坝

China International Travel Service (CITS)
Kunming Branch
Huancheng Nan Lu
tel. 24992, tx. 64027,
cable 3266 KUNMING
中国国际旅行社昆明分社

China Travel Service (CTS)
Kunming Branch
Huancheng Nan Lu
tel. 24992, tx. 64027,
cable 3266 KUNMING
中国旅行社昆明分社

Kunming Railway Station
Nanyao (southern end of Beijing Lu)
Inquiries tel. 22321
Baggage tel. 25469
昆明火车站　南窑

Kunming Taxi Company
Jinri Gongyuan (opposite Kunming Department Store)
tel. 26243
昆明市汽车出租公司　近日公园

Kunming Three-wheeled Taxi Service
45 Beijing Lu
tel. 23389
昆明机场三轮车队　北京路45号

Miscellaneous

Chinese Academy of Sciences
Kunming Branch
Huguo Lu
tel. 24347
中国科学院昆明分院　护国路

Kunming Brewery
Bailongtan, Bei Jiao
tel. 26662
昆明啤酒厂　北郊白龙潭

Kunming Institute of Botany
Heilongtan, Bei Jiao
tel. 24053, 24197
昆明植物研究所　北郊黑龙潭

Kunming Institute of Zoology
Huahongdong, Xi Jiao
tel. 81743
昆明动物研究所　西郊花红洞

Kunming Islamic Association
51 Zhengyi Lu
昆明市伊斯兰教协会　正义路51号

Yunnan Provincial Library
Cuihu Nan Lu
tel. 27357, 23960
云南省图书馆　翠湖南路

Yunnan College of Arts
101 Mayuan
tel. 23080
云南艺术学院　麻园101号

Yunnan Foreign Trade Bureau
113 Huashan Nan Lu
tel. 28175, tx. 64023
云南对外贸易局　华山南路113号

**Yunnan Provincial Agricultural
Exhibition Hall**
Cuihu Bei Lu
云南省农业展览馆　翠湖北路

**Yunnan Provincial Gymnasium and
Sports Complex**
Dongfeng Dong Lu
tel. 24037
云南省体育馆　东风东路

Yunnan University
52 Cuihu Bei Lu
tel. 23901, 23232
云南大学　翠湖北路52号

Index of Places